WHY I GO TO MASS

Reflections by Catholic Parishioners

ST. MARY OF SORROWS PARISH

Why I Go to Mass
Reflections of the Parishioners of St. Mary of Sorrows
Copyright © 2022 St.Mary of Sorrows Roman Catholic Church

Published in the United States of America

Cover design by K.B. Owen
Cover photograph by Susan Lee

"But there are also many other things which Jesus did; were every one of them to be written, I suppose that the world itself could not contain the books that would be written."

— JOHN 21:35

Why Do We Go To Mass?

A PREFACE BY

REVEREND JAMES S. BARKETT, PASTOR

"For where two or three are gathered in My name, there I am in the midst of them."

— *MATTHEW 18:20*

In this chaotic, broken world, and especially as we emerged from a pandemic which greatly restricted Mass attendance, I have been inspired by the numbers of people coming to Mass, on weekends and even daily. I KNOW why I come to Mass - but I began to wonder why others do. I asked our Blessed Mother and Patroness, Our Lady of Sorrows, "Why do people come?" And she told me: why not just ask THEM! So, I did.

THIS BOOKLET IS A COMPILATION OF THE RESPONSES BY parishioners of St Mary of Sorrows Catholic Church to my question to them "Why do you come to Mass?" We have anonymized the inputs, and have attempted to loosely organize them into broad groupings. There is one section that captures responses that touch on the tragedy of sexual abuse both within the Church and in our families. These responses deserve, no … demand … inclusion, because to not include them would be a disservice to all those who have experienced pain and who thirst for the peace and security only found with Our Lord.

WE HAVE INCLUDED AT THE END SOME RESOURCES YOU MAY find helpful in answering questions that these stories and inputs may have generated, along with where you may obtain information about renewing your Catholic faith, assisting others to explore becoming Catholic, and becoming more involved with your fellow Parishioners.

I THANK ALL THE PARISHIONERS AND OTHERS WHO TOOK THE time and made the effort to respond to my question and all those who helped me usher this project from initial thought to this booklet you hold in your hands. I am privileged to be supported by a wonderful Parish.

I PRAY YOU MAY BE INSPIRED BY THESE LIFE STORIES AND responses about how going to Mass has become more than an obligation. Please pray about how YOU might answer the question if asked. And please share these ideas, stories, and thoughts with someone you know who doesn't come to Mass as often as they might.

I HOPE YOU FIND THE JOY, AND PEACE, AND MOTIVATION TO continue to grow in the Catholic faith. May God bless you.

Reverend James S. Barkett
Pastor, St Mary of Sorrows Church
Fairfax, VA

Families

"We love, because He first loved us."

— *1 JOHN 4:19*

In today's fast paced and stress filled world, I find reassurance and encouragement that there still exists a place of hope and kindness when I attend Mass. Just the simple act of being in God's presence and receiving Him through the Eucharist gives me a sense of recharge that I can take on the week with a positive outlook. No matter the crosses that I might face, I know that I can simply return the next week and get past my trouble. When I hear the songs of praise, receive an offering of peace from a parishioner, or sit in quiet reflection, I find it is refreshing to end a week and start the next with these and other moments I can only get while attending Mass. Though my life has changed from being a teenager, young adult, husband, and father, I have found that the Church is always a source where I can find ways to provide for my spiritual and physical needs.

I go to Mass because:

- My Dad takes me.
- I love Jesus.
- People are nice to me.

As a boy my parents instilled faith into our daily lives, like saying grace at dinner. My sisters and I were close in age, and we attended church every Sunday. I remember one Sunday when we were living in Newport, Rhode Island. As Mass was at the base church, they had several services of different denominations. There had been a recent switch in Mass times, so we showed up for the 10 a.m. Mass. We sat in the front pew. When Mass began my father realized it was a Protestant service. We stood up and walked out while the preacher kept saying, "Please come back and sit." We ran down the aisle.

We moved six different times during my father's time in the service. The second church we attended was St. Bernadette's. That was from 1971 to 1973. Back then it was a small church, not like it is now. Then we moved back to Newport from 1973 to 1974. We attended St. Mary's Roman Catholic Church. It is a beautiful church. It was the same church in which John and Jackie Kennedy were married in 1953. It's the oldest church in the Providence Diocese. Mom joined the choir there.

On Christmas Day 1973, we went to midnight Mass. Mom and the choir sounded beautiful. The following summer we moved to San Diego. The church, Carmel Mountain Christian Church, had not been built yet so all the Masses were held in a country club dining room. The priest, Father

Nicholas, was an imposing man of 6'5". He loved to roll your knuckles when he shook your hand. I became an altar boy during the summer of 1975. It didn't last long. I fell asleep and missed the bell. After Mass he took me aside and said, "I can't have you falling asleep during Mass." I resigned.

We moved here in the summer of 1976. Our first Mass at St. Mary's was held in Robinson High School. One of the funniest things happened during the Christmas Mass of 1976. Father Farrell came from behind the partition and as he moved along the stage he stumbled and he said, "Too much of the sacrificial wine!" Everyone laughed. In 1994 my grandmother moved in with us. Every Sunday she and I would attend Mass. She really liked Father Casey. When he passed away, she did not want to go anymore. I started attending church on a regular basis in 2015 after my dad passed. I joined the Knights in 2017.

Now on why I come to church. I love coming to hear the priests and deacons talk about God and to hear their jokes and stories. I love greeting people at the door. I love being an usher. Coming to Mass fills me up with hope. I don't see much of that outside those doors. I haven't had the greatest life. I have hope, however, that things will get better. They have to, right?

WHEN I WAS A LITTLE GIRL, MY FAVORITE MASS TO ATTEND was the Christmas Eve Mass. For many years of my childhood, I participated in the children's Christmas pageant at St. James Catholic Church in Falls Church, Virginia. My 8th grade year, I even had the privilege of playing the Blessed Mother, and I got to hold a real baby (which was terrifying to me at age 13!).

I remember how beautiful the church was on Christmas Eve, all decorated with poinsettias, evergreen, and holly. It was always dark when we arrived, and then light filled the church and the sound of trumpets filled the air from the choir loft as Mass began and we all stood to sing. I loved the scent of the candles and the atmosphere of excitement and holiness. How wonderful it was to see families together and the church filled, with standing room only. Those experiences of fullness, light, beauty, worship, of love itself, will stay with me always, and it's what I imagine Heaven to be like.

In full disclosure, as a girl, I was also excited for Mass to finish on Christmas Eve, so we could get to my grandmother's house for presents, KFC chicken, and to drink punch from the fancy punch bowl and glasses!

When I was in college, I would stop into church after my classes or just when I needed the quiet that only Jesus can offer. Walking into church always felt like home base, and I'm forever grateful to my parents for raising my sisters and me with this foundation.

As an adult, one of my favorite memories is of visiting Old Saint Mary's Cathedral in San Francisco, California. I remember feeling such a connection with the Lord and with the Body of Christ - all believers - despite being so far from home. That's what being part of the Church, the Body of Christ, means to me - connecting to God and others - following Jesus and taking part in His Kingdom's work - saying yes to Him - trusting Him when I can't see ahead in times of suffering, mine and that of others, and to believing Him, His Word as Truth.

When I attend Mass now, in my 50's, I feel connected to God, other believers, and to myself from every life stage, as well as to my family, culture, and history. Being part of the history that began with Jesus is an extraordinary feeling of connection in the vast and ever-changing world.

Sometimes, I overthink it. I ponder and analyze all the questions. But Jesus simply says, "Be still and know that I am God." During Mass, I'm able to lift my voice with other believers in worship. I experience Jesus in the Word, and it's Him who invites us to His table, to remember His love for us, His sacrificial suffering and death for our salvation, to remember He's with us always, Our Immanuel.

That's what I'll be thinking about this Christmas as I remember with great fondness the Christmas Eve Masses from my childhood - Jesus with us, our Immanuel, the Light in the Darkness.

Why I Go to Mass: A family's response

Dad - I was raised Catholic and attended Catholic schools until college. At that point, my faith had not been an internal or personal one - Mass and prayers were what I was supposed to do. After college, I took to pursuing the world's "finer things" in life, participated in the more "exciting" events and adventures available to a single professional in Washington D.C. The dating and all the "doing" I thought was great fun and filled my time, but the more I "did" the more I felt I needed to do. I needed to find the next something awesome and fulfilling that I had not yet encountered. The adventures became more grandiose, seeking the bigger better deal, pushing beyond the limits of my physical body. Beside the "accomplishment: did it, check that box" nothing felt really fulfilling - aside from having great "bragging rights" stories to tell during more empty social events.

As the activities began to hit the "peak" of physical, psychological and encounter extremes, I had gradually begun attending Masses that happened to be celebrated by priests who were good homilists. I also cannot discount the continuous prayers by my amazing parents and my mother's consecration of me to Mary - out of frustration for her very frustrating son. It was in hearing my faith through the scriptures and poignant/pointed homilies that the almost extinguished ember of my own Catholic faith was fanned, moving from barely smoldering to a self-realization of being Catholic.

How did this happen? As with Bartimaeus, Jesus was passing by and Bartimaeus called out to Him. Bartimaeus called out because he wanted Jesus, not the things of the world which he had and decided they were not all that. Jesus, too, had passed by me so many times in my life. He always quietly invited, but I was always too busy to pay attention. In all those "adventures and experiences," He kept passing by me. I saw Him and mostly ignored Him. It wasn't a moment in my life where I was struck down in some tragic event, but in my emptiness, amidst all the busyness, that I called out to Jesus - "Jesus, thank you for all you have done for me. I am a sinner; help me to seek you, long for you, love you, trust you and have the faith that you are in everyone and everything. Help me to seek you above all things - especially above all that this world offers: the fine foods, tantalizing experiences and adventures, pleasures of the body and the spirit."

My faith journey is like going to the beach. Most of my life, I thought things were great, but I was still in the parking lot at the beach. As I learned more about my faith, I gradually moved closer to the ocean. For a long time, I have been standing in the shallows, just up to my knees. Sometimes I jump in, other times I swim, but I mostly stand in the shallows. Mother Mary is always inviting me to know Jesus more. My willingness to go to Mass is my act of love for God and the desire to want to be strengthened through receiving Jesus in the Eucharist. This is also part of my faith journey, my desire to go out deeper into the ocean, where things are not as chaotic as the shallows: God's Ocean of love for us - His mystery and awesomeness. The Mass is my chance to say, "Thank you" for all His mercy and blessings, to say, "I am sorry" for my offenses and failings, to ask for forgiveness and strength to start again, to trust in Jesus and God's greater plan.

Mom - I am blessed to have been born into a marvelous Catholic family with German and Irish roots. My parents have been married for over 50 years and continue to love one another deeply! When I was 15, I remember thinking, "I really don't want to go to Mass unless God is real." This question stayed with me and soon after, I attended a winter youth retreat. I was by myself in my room, looking out onto the Atlantic Ocean. I have always found the ocean breathtaking and wondered, "Is God more powerful than this ocean?" I had my bible with me and on a whim, I just opened it to a random page. My eyes fell on these words in the Psalms: "More powerful than the breakers on high is the Lord God Almighty." I was astounded to experience God's presence and was filled with gratitude.

Fast forward to my mid-20's. I was attending a young adult conference where I went to a workshop on the Eucharist. Surprisingly, the speaker asked us about our experiences during mealtimes, our cultures and what meal times meant to us. She went on to say that we share our very selves with one another as we eat meals together. It was as if I were discovering for the first time how profound a gift the Eucharist is. Then, she began to invite us into a deeper understanding of what it means that Christ comes to us in and through a Meal and gives us Himself as food.

Around this same time, I stopped after work to attend Mass at the parish I belonged to in downtown Baltimore. I immediately noticed a guest priest, who shared that he was visiting from Africa. After the Mass was over, he kindly asked us all for a favor, "Would you all mind staying for a moment for a picture? Today is my 15-year anniversary of the priesthood and you, the Church, are my bride." As I got up and took my place in this picture with the group of parishioners and this priest, I felt an outpouring of grace and gratitude. This was a window into the beauty of the body of Christ and the relationship between the priests and the people they serve. Now as a wife and mom, I continue to experience God strengthening and nourishing our marriage and family life in the Eucharist.

16-YEAR-OLD - I GO TO MASS TO REMEMBER AND THANK GOD for His sacrifice that we see in the Eucharist. By attending Mass, we show Him our love and devotion. I also see attending Mass as a way for my family to grow even more with love for each other.

15-YEAR-OLD - EACH SUNDAY, THE SACRIFICE OF THE MASS happens. It is the most powerful thing I can do as a Catholic. I, along with the entire congregation, come together and worship Jesus and receive Him, Body, Blood, Soul, and Divinity. I go to Mass to grow closer to God, my Rock, and to receive Him each Sunday. I try my best to truly believe that God is present there. I love the fact that even though everyone's lives are crazy and distracting, every seven days, every Sunday, we get to relive Jesus' life, death, and resurrection, and we get to profess our faith and receive Him into our body and soul as eternal nourishment.

13-YEAR-OLD - I GO TO MASS BECAUSE JESUS IS TRULY present in it. During the Mass, we receive the holy sacrament of the Holy Eucharist. We need Jesus because He is the reason we are here today. There is this saying that the angels are perfectly content in Heaven, except that they are jealous that we get to receive Jesus' Body and Blood in the Eucharist. The Mass is a gift. We might as well use it.

9-YEAR-OLD - I GO TO MASS BECAUSE I LOVE GOD AND I LOVE to receive Holy Communion. Sometimes, I don't feel like going to Mass, but I go anyway with my family. I enjoy it because I am with them and it makes me comfortable. Also, I go to Mass because I love Jesus and I want to accept what He gives us. I want to love Him and I want to be with Him in heaven forever.

AS A DAILY PROCEDURE IN THE EARLY MORNING, I READ sections of the Bible, study scripture, pray for my family members and others in need. I communicate with the Lord and can feel His presence.

During the holy Mass, the presence of the Lord is not only verbally present, but physically present as well.

The biblical readings, the singing of the Mass, the transformation of the bread and wine, the Holy Eucharist, all confirm a physical presence.

WHY DO WE GO TO MASS? BECAUSE IT IS THE RIGHT THING TO do. Jesus told us to. Because we are Catholic. That was a good reason when we were young. Now not so much.

Jesus is present at the Mass. Jesus whose Father is Love. Jesus who loves us. Mass is a community of people who have come to touch our Lord and Savior. If only I touch Him; if only I welcome Him into my heart, into my soul…

Christ gave His life for us. He welcomes us into His house.

But once I was not so much in love.

When I was young, we attended Mass as a family. Yet in college sleep was more important, and later I was too busy. Yet there was an aching, even when attending a church of another tradition. We married in the Church, but still enjoyed Sunday doing other things.

Then came children and now we are a family, and we experienced a new love.

So, we went to Mass and were filled with the Holy Spirit. And the journey is sweeter every day.

We know Jesus.

I MAKE EVERY EFFORT TO ATTEND MASS WEEKLY WITH MY WIFE and three children. It is during Mass that I feel closest to God through prayer, scripture, and song.

It is also important to me to set a good example and foundation for my children.

IN MY MIND ON SUNDAYS, I AM 'RUNNING' TOWARD MASS TO meet Jesus at the door, at His house. He has invited me over to participate in receiving His gifts, and I don't want to miss out! I am prepared to participate by pre-reading the readings and psalms.

I am bringing (spiritually) with me two of my closest friends, my sons who have fallen away from the faith. I pray for my parents who have passed away. So much is remembrance and love.

I pray that I'll be a better Christian to my family and those I meet along the way. I am trying to walk with Jesus and it's been a lifelong journey.

THE WORLD IS LOUD.

The world is busy.

The world is filled with distractions.

SUNDAY COMES.

Quick shower.

Chug coffee.

Wrangle kids out of pjs.

Pack snacks.

Ask for the 5th time for the "big" kids to put their shoes on.

Did we bring the baby's pacifier?

Wrestle kids into car seats.

SIT, BREATHE, SMILE AT JESUS.

Hush kids.

Give snacks.

Hear God's word.

Breathe again.

Rock baby.

Take toddler out.

Hear a beautiful pearl of insight from Father's homily.

Sit back down with family.

Feel wave of gratitude.

CONSECRATION.

Witness a miracle.

Hold sticky toddler's hand as you walk up to receive Jesus.

Feel His warm embrace.

Feel His love.

Receive His grace.

Feel His peace.

Mass is rest.
A new start.
A needed embrace.
It's grace giving.
A reminder I am and will forever be a beloved daughter
of God.

I GO TO MASS IN RESPONSE TO GOD'S CALLING TO ME. FROM A
very young age, I have been aware of His calling to me. Fast
forward to the pandemic…on August 19, 2020, through St.
Padre Pio, God called our family to become parishioners of
St. Mary of Sorrows Catholic Church. The calling was excep-
tionally bright and quite spectacular to the eyes! Although I
had not anticipated a call of this fantastical magnitude from
Him on that particular summer day, I think I wasn't totally
surprised, as God is always calling me.

After my eyes had adjusted from all the brightness, I drove
home from the St. Padre Pio relics/presentation at St. Mary
of Sorrows Church, pondering on what had just happened to
me. I quickly found the parish registration form online. The
next day, I conferred with my family and completed the parish
registration form. The next day, I submitted the form to the
parish office, and we became parishioners of St. Mary of
Sorrows Catholic Church that day…all in response to His call.
We are so thankful for His calling us, and as St. Augustine
said, "…our hearts are restless until they rest in You."

WHY DO I GO TO MASS? THE SHORT ANSWER - BECAUSE
Jesus draws me there to give Himself to me: Body, Blood, Soul
and Divinity in the Eucharist.

But how I got to that point takes a little longer…

A three-year-old girl holds her Daddy's hand as they walk into church to make a "visit" to pray for healing after an eye doctor appointment. Church, Mass - that was the backbone of our family life.

A seven-year-old hears Sister Lucienne say, "Your First Holy Communion Day will be one of the happiest in your life." Receiving Jesus, truly, really present, into my heart was incredible. I was in awe! Some say that a seven-year-old can't appreciate the fullness of the Eucharist. I disagree.

A seventeen-year-old goes away to college at a huge, public university after twelve years of Catholic school. "You'll lose your faith!" my counselor said. And though I struggled and wrestled with faith at first, it was Jesus in the Eucharist who continued to draw me - to the Catholic student chapel, eventually to daily Mass, and to a strong community, some of whom remain my best friends fifty years later.

A twenty-eight-year-old new mom just lost both of her brothers in a car accident. It was at Mass, and especially in the Eucharist, that I found consolation and peace.

Four children in six years, always someone fussing at Sunday Mass, hard to concentrate. Long commute to work - no daily Mass. It was a dry time, but Jesus was there waiting.

Finally, an empty nester and remembering how life was always better when I was able to go to daily Mass. First a couple of days per week, then more, until it became an everyday choice - and I <u>miss</u> Him when for some reason I cannot go.

Jesus is always there for me - in the words of the readings or the prayers, and always under the appearances of bread and wine in the Eucharist. He is waiting for me, drawing me to Himself.

How can I say no?

That's why I go to Mass.

✣

It is hard to get my family together for anything except Mass when they are in town.

We managed a family dinner with the question of why we go to Mass and they shared the following:

Dad: it's a commandment; it is so important to God that He commands us to keep His day holy.

One son shared that he comes to Mass to be a part of a community that serves God and serves others.

His wife, our daughter-in-law, shared that fellowship with all people is important to her.

Another son added, worship with the community is why he is present.

My addition to the above is that receiving Jesus in the Eucharist, the source and summit of our faith, is why I come. Years ago, a priest told me the more we receive Jesus, the more we become like Him. I want to be like Jesus! I love being a part of the Body of Christ and knowing that Jesus loves me despite my human flaws. I also love being at Mass with our grandsons, sharing our faith with them and seeing the awe in their faces as they look at the beautiful new church and hear the choir and liturgical music.

Thank you for this opportunity to share and have this discussion within our family. Maybe a weekly question for family conversation is in order. This gave an opportunity to evangelize within our family that we would not have had otherwise.

As with anything we experience, our answers to these types of questions change over the years. When I was little, in elementary school, I went to Mass with my family; it was never a question, just part of who we were. The whole family got dressed up and I loved it because I wasn't in a school uniform, so I could choose what to wear for a great celebration. Instead of a birthday party, I was celebrating Jesus and being part of something so much bigger that my immediate family. It may sound superficial, but we are going to meet the King of Kings.

During my teen years, I went to Mass as a part of service to my Parish as I was a Lector and EM for the Youth Mass. Participating in the Liturgy in these special ways gave me a place to feel helpful and fulfill a duty to serve others before myself – I've always been a "Martha girl." During my college years, I found comfort and consolation in attending daily Mass to really get to know Jesus and have an inner peace when the outside world was demanding so many decisions to be made. This is when I found the "Mary" in me: "sitting by the feet of Jesus." Throughout my 20's and 30's, the Eucharist brought me to Mass each week, despite my busy lifestyle. I knew I needed to receive Jesus in such an intimate way in order to face the week ahead. I once heard during a talk that "Grace was like Gatorade for the Soul," and I was very thirsty as a young adult trying to live in a culture that was so different from what I believed. This was the first time I really had to stand up for Christ. Being at Mass and Adoration gave me the fortitude to be that child of God.

Now, as a parent, my reasoning is two-fold: lead by example and extend my personal relationship with Jesus. I want my children to have the same joy and appreciation I grew up with going to Mass and experiencing Jesus in so many ways, but I also know I can't do it for them: they will find their own path to Jesus. My intentions at Mass are always for my children to "want" to be at Mass. So, prayer is a big reason why I attend Mass; not only is it a dedicated time, it is the greatest prayer as it is Our Lord's invitation to us to be with Him.

Many people will say, I don't have time for this or that and Mass becomes part of that conversation. That is simply not an option for me. I love sports and to be good at it, one must practice. The same is true about going to Mass. Yes, I have all the (plays) prayers memorized and can go through the motions, but will I get the same euphoric feeling (hitting the game winning basket) receiving Jesus if I'm only doing the bare minimum, just showing up? It takes effort and desire to be better than the last time. I want to have that special Jesus time with me as much as possible.

My son once expressed his sentiments about going to Mass this way: "If the God of the Universe is willing to meet me at Mass every day, who am I to say I'm too busy?" I agree with him...there is nothing more meaningful than Mass.

I go to Mass from guidance from my father. When I was about six or seven, I groused about going to Mass "every Sunday" when my neighbor (who was Protestant) only went to church "occasionally." My dad explained that there are 168 hours in a week and the small time going to Mass, "about an hour," was the least we could do to follow our faith.

THANK YOU FOR ASKING THIS QUESTION, BECAUSE I REALIZE the answer has evolved over time. I was raised by a daughter of Irish Catholic immigrants. Three of my grandfather's brothers were priests. We were raised to attend Mass out of a strict sense of obligation, more than anything else. As children, we resisted, but resistance was futile. I also attended Catholic school through fourth grade, so early on I developed some intellectual and moral sense of the importance of adhering to the Church's teachings. But my primary motivations were obedience and obligation.

By junior high school I had developed enough of a sense of dedication that I became an altar server, and during the summers I would walk to daily Mass just to get better at being an altar server. Mass was a thing I did because I believed it to be important to practice my religion as I was taught. I even considered studying to be a priest, but ultimately decided that my talents (and what God had made me to do) lay elsewhere. That sense of dedication – and obligation – continued into high school. So, I think at that stage my motivation was also out of a sense of procedure and duty.

In college I joined the Catholic Choir and met a friend who went to Mass with me, and as roommates for a year after college we went to Mass together. That was the first time in my life I experienced going to a Mass as a thing to share with a friend rather than an obligation to participate in with the family. Thus, friendship and musical participation became my motivation.

In the Navy, going to Mass became a secondary part of my life, for a couple of reasons. Duties made it difficult to attend Mass regularly, and that disrupted schedule undermined the motivation to attend even when I had the weekend off. Moreover, for a short time I was married to a non-

Catholic under a special dispensation, and her disrespect for my faith made practicing it even more difficult.

Once I had separated from my first wife (ultimately annulled), I decided that it was important that any woman I dated be Catholic because I realized how fundamental my religion was to my life. I was fortunate to find a woman who had kindled an enthusiasm for the Church at Lasalle College among the Christian Brothers. We regularly participated in Mass together at St. Thomas Aquinas on the campus of the University of Connecticut where the Paulists made us feel very welcome and further inspired a sense of community and connection. So, at that stage in my life, I was attending Mass out of love and a sense of connection, particularly from a heightened awareness of the union through the Eucharist with Christ and thereby with the Church.

I had something of a revelation at my grandfather's funeral Mass, when I realized how immediately relevant the weekly celebration of the Resurrection over the course of my life became in that specific celebration of my grandfather's transition from death to life. Celebrating the Mass that day rang with a strong sense of familiarity, so that, in a way, it all made more sense. From that point on, my participation in the Mass became a more conscious celebration of hope for the Resurrection, as well as a connection not only with the Church on earth but with the communion of saints in Heaven, one that transcended the separation we experience at the death of a family member. That feeling came even more strongly at my mother's funeral years later.

When we originally came to Saint Mary of Sorrows, we were a bit overwhelmed by the size of the community and felt "isolated in the crowd." It wasn't until later, when we started participating in some of the ministries – my wife as a Eucharistic Minister and me as a catechist and later as a lector – that we started to feel the same connection in the physical community of the parish I knew abstractly was present in the spiritual communion but had struggled to foster in daily and weekly awareness.

So today we come to Mass in what has become a gradually cultivated, mature confluence of all those reasons: obedience, duty, love, community, and hope. In a way, we come to Mass because we've always come to Mass – not that we haven't had our lapses and crises of faith, but just because well, it's home, and home is where the heart is.

FOR MY WIFE AND ME, THE MORE PERTINENT QUESTION becomes "Why wouldn't we go to Mass?"

Weekly attendance at Mass is simply continuing what I have done from the youngest age I can remember. I was raised Presbyterian, but weekly church and Sunday school was just what we did as a family. It was non-negotiable. From my senior year in high school and for the next year or so, I relegated the Lord to the back seat in the events of my life. Fortunately, the Lord made himself known to me in a way that I recall vividly to this day. That was the beginning of God taking the reins and leading me gradually to a life far different from what I had conceived or wanted at that time.

I could always sense when the Lord was working in my life. I would feel Him drawing me away from my desires or life plans that were not within His will, and my response seemed to be always one of opposition to that. I did not easily surrender to God.

Along the way I started attending Catholic Mass, even before I was Catholic. I did not receive communion, yet I would go into a Catholic church and feel the Lord in a way that I never had in a Protestant church. I didn't know what it all meant, but there was no mistaking the experience of Christ there. From that point on, through my relationship with my wife-to-be, I had my intellectual difficulties with Catholicism resolved (primarily the real presence of Christ in the Eucharist). I was confirmed into the Catholic Church two months before we were married in that same church.

Now, having lived most of my life, I attend not only Mass weekly, but daily. My original excuse that daily Mass would probably make the Eucharist seem too ordinary was totally inaccurate. Instead of taking it for granted, I consider it to be my spiritual strength that helps me get through the day.

MASS HAS BEEN IMPRINTED INTO ME SINCE MY EARLIEST DAYS and it has become an essential part of my well-being.

My mother took my brother and me to Sunday Mass regularly from the age of three because we were trying to show a good example to my father, who was not a Catholic at that time. We went to a Catholic grade school that had Mass on special holy days and every First Friday. Then, when I was nine, I was selected to become an altar boy who served Mass at our parish. My father helped me to learn the Latin responses and this was the first time I felt really special as a person. I watched the priests carefully from fifth grade to the end of eighth grade.

After eighth grade, I thought I wanted to be a priest…and signed up for the minor seminary. So, attendance at daily Mass became an essential part of every day for the next six-plus years. I was even selected to be trained as a Master of Ceremonies and learned the details of how to serve at all types of celebrations of Mass: weddings, funerals, and especially Masses when the bishop presides ("Solemn-High" Masses). I felt so special for being allowed to do those things, and the bishop called on our "pontifical crew" several times per year at different parishes. I studied the Mass, loved the Mass, loved having a responsible position, and was required to teach

other seminarians how to serve at all kinds of liturgical celebrations.

By age 20, I had all of this imprinted on my being, and I
enjoyed all types of church celebrations, much like I enjoyed
playing sports and learning foreign languages. Then I left
seminary, finished college, got married, joined the Air Force,
stopped going to daily Mass, but always attended Sunday and
Holy Day Masses and helped the Catholic Chaplains wherever we were stationed. When the Church approved lay
readers (Lectors) at Mass, I was among the first to volunteer.
When Extraordinary Ministers of Holy Communion were
allowed, I was, again, among the first to volunteer as I
believed it was my duty, as a former seminarian, to be active in
Church activities. Now, after more than 50 years, I still feel the
same. My wife and I taught all six children the importance of
Mass, as Jesus' sacrifice for us, and Jesus' gift to us of His own
Body and Blood at Mass. Most of them "got it."

As a Senior citizen I feel the need to be refreshed by the
Eucharist--and Mass is the duty, the place where that happens!
I want to be there at least once per week, if not more often.
The Mass feels like an integral part of my personality and life
experience. I WANT to be there to thank God for all the
blessings He has showered on our Family, and for the physical
and spiritual healings He has worked in my life.

MY FAMILY AND I GO TO MASS TO BE WITH JESUS. IT IS THAT
simple. Worshiping the Lord is what we all expect to do on
Sunday. This formal worship with our parish gives our lives
direction and a purpose.

Although our weekdays are filled with multiple overlap-
ping schedules, Mass reminds us of a bigger routine going on
in our lives - our journey to heaven. God knows we have a
long way to go and that we require many stops in the confes-

sional, but He is kind and merciful. He is not bothered by the noise and disturbances we caused when our children were all under five years old. He is not bothered when we are not in the most prayerful mood as we walk through the church doors. He takes us where we are and speaks tenderly to us and feeds us selflessly and generously. As a good Dad, He knows what we need, and He always provides.

Our family takes up less pew space now as some of our children have gone off to college. Now it is their turn to make the personal decision to be with the Lord on Sundays for Mass and maybe a few weekdays, as schedules allow. They are finding that God's comfort and peace always reminds them that they have a home in our Church and in the Mass.

WITH THE FULL REALIZATION THAT THIS IS FOR NON-attribution at least until the final judgement day...

I have gone to Mass for many reasons throughout the phases of my life. Through 12 years of Catholic school, I went because that was what we did. Raised in an Irish-Catholic family of first generation non-NYPD/FDNY parents, when mother said it was time for church and we all piled into the back of the station wagon. Once I was old enough, like the rest of my brothers, I became an altar server. Then, we were scheduled for Masses, like it or not. The saving grace was that after weekday morning Masses, we got to practice driving the stick shift in the empty school/church parking lot.

After parochial schools, I was institutionalized again, this time in "Uncle Sam's Home for Wayward Boys on the Hudson"; also known as West Point. Mass was the one time of the week where no one bothered you. Mass was my connection to family and home that didn't exist in any other ritual or tradition. God didn't judge the shine on your shoes or the tuck on your shirt; he just wanted you there for who you could become.

Moving on to the next phase, I tried adulting on my own. Assigned overseas, there were distractions that tempted me and weekends were short. I drifted a bit, maybe not as regular a church-goer as I could have been. Before I left, though, I met a nice Catholic girl who re invigorated my interest and in the Mass, too. That began the shared interest as we worked on our lives and faith together.

Then, we entered the child-rearing years. What made this phase most interesting is that, unknown at the time, I had married a serial volunteer. She was up for anything the church had going. Using the philosophy of divide and conquer, she did the church stuff and I did the kid stuff. Before getting 10,000 steps per day was fashionable, I walked various children through, around, and all over the church property during services. I knew where every bathroom, quiet room and playground within a quarter mile of every church we attended. Gradually, the children grew up with a mix of Catholic schools and secular schools -Jesuits, Carmelites, Europa-Schule, St. James, depending where we were. And there were weekday and weekend morning Masses with new altar servers. My mom may not have seen many birthdays or graduations, but she was there for every sacrament during her lifetime.

Now we're in a different place. I go to Mass for us; just for us. Maybe it's looking at mortality up close and personal. Maybe it's the closeness it brings us to share our faith without all the distractions. So, this phase seems to be ready to last a while, at least until we have grandchildren to walk through, around and all over church properties again.

Cradle Catholics

"Do whatever He tells you."

— JOHN 2:5

Like every Catholic, I know the answer to the question, "Why do you go to Sunday Mass?" Because it's a mortal sin not to go! But that's not the answer I'm giving today.

Several years ago, a young woman's dying request to my Catholic friend was that she pray the rosary. She said, "Pray the whole rosary, Mary Ann; the mysteries, the accompanying Bible verse and the fruits of each mystery." My friend shared that conversation with me which, in turn, started me on my own rosary journey. And what a trip it has been!

I'm ashamed to admit that as a devout cradle Catholic, when I prayed, I'd make my requests known, but never really expected much in the way of an answer from God. So, it was with this mindset I began to say my rosary. I wasn't really expecting much from Our Lady. Little did I know! As time passed, I noticed I was talking to the Holy Spirit all day long (1st Luminous-Openness to the Holy Spirit) and I had such a strong desire to be holy (4th Luminous-Desire for Holiness). "Why am I so focused on being holy?" I remembered thinking. my personal daily prayer was that I 'Do whatever He tells you', as the Blessed Mother told the servants at the Wedding at Cana (2nd Luminous-To Jesus through Mary.) It was like Our Lady had lifted the "veil" from these mysteries I'd known my whole life and let me really see them for the first time. They took on such deep meaning for me.

I **wanted** to be obedient to all Church teachings (4th Joyful-Obedience) and began to focus on where I might be falling short. I started trying to make First Saturday devotions and confession every month. Meditating on the Sorrowful mysteries, which have always been most dear to me, became so much more intense. I began to pray to the Shoulder Wound of Jesus which I never knew was His most painful wound. The Glorious mysteries have given me such tremendous gratitude for what God has done and continues to do for me that my heart overflows with love for Him. This deep love led me to start attending daily Mass. If the Mass is the highest form of prayer, then I wanted to be a part of that prayer. It has become such a part of my life that if I can't physically attend Mass, I watch it on YouTube. (My husband does too!) Receiving Communion has become more important to me than ever before. To think that I hold in my hand and take into my body God Himself is just too powerful to comprehend and yet everyday He lets me do just that! How can I ever do enough to thank God for His great goodness to me?

So why do I really "go to Sunday Mass?" Because I **want** to go. I want to thank the Blessed Mother for gently leading me closer to her Son, and to show my love and gratitude to God in the best way I can for all the love He gives me.

✠

WHY DO I GO TO MASS? THAT IS A QUESTION I HAVE ASKED myself in the past, back when I was in college for the first year. And, the answer is always "My mom." What does that mean?

Well, I can go on and on and on, but briefly, I will try to explain.

First, I am a "cradle Catholic", a term I do not really appreciate, but know that people understand it to mean I have always been Catholic, raised in a Catholic church-going family, who sent us to Catholic schools for our (I am the oldest of 4 siblings) entire grade school careers.

My family was "poor" by most American standards, living in a small 4 room (yes, 4 rooms total: living room, kitchen, and 2 bedrooms) wood frame home in South Texas, where my dad was the major bread-winner as a blue-collar civil service worker. We were "poor," but never wanted for any essentials, other than the times the hurricanes left our house out of power. But, even then, we were able to stand in line to get free peanut butter, bread, cheese…everything we needed to get by until the electricity was restored.

God was good. That is what I grew up learning. I always believed in God and Jesus, but did not truly understand the meaning of the Trinity until high school. The Sisters of the Incarnate Word in South Texas made sure of that. The Trinity is and always will be a mystery that you believe through faith. But, as long as you establish a relationship with the second person of this Trinity – Jesus – then that is all that really matters.

We lived poorly, but we had everything we needed: loving, devoted parents, a good Catholic education, and the living essentials (more than most third world countries can claim).

That is not to say that our family was the ideal family. My dad was an alcoholic and there were times I remember loud disagreements between my parents as my drunk father again made his way out with the boys to the local bar, my mom pleading for him to stay. He claimed he needed to relax, unwind; you know the story. Her prayers gave her the strength to carry on, and although it was a tough life for her, she gave her all to make certain we had the best possible upbringing she and my father could give us.

And, even so, my devoted Dad provided for and was completely loyal and selfless to my mother and his four children. I won't ever forget the pony rides on his back, and how he loved to show us how to play poker, blackjack, and even dice and dominoes. We children all continue to love playing games of all kinds. Just for fun, mind you.

We went through some tough economic times, when we had to make do with rice and beans as meals for weeks, but my mom never failed to show us that, despite the meager times, we could always give to those in need, when we had enough. There were some elderly neighbors who lived next door to us. He was a retired fisherman, and she was a homemaker, raising their grandchild alone, as the daughter had run off. I remember taking them nice big plates for every major holiday – Thanksgiving, Christmas, Easter, and even Memorial Day. We always had at least enough for an extra plate or two for them. Miraculous, isn't it? Like the old lady from the Bible, with the last few drops of oil and a handful of flour, which lasted her a year.

You see, I always remember my childhood as a very happy childhood. One full of love, faith and miracles, yes, miracles.

Like the one where a small jar of baby food appeared in our cabinet, only after my mom prayed fervently that it would, for her hungry, crying baby boy (my youngest sibling). Only on the third try of my baby sister opening the cabinet (upon my mom's third hope-filled prayer request), did the baby food jar appear to my mom's great relief, so she could get my little brother fed, so he would stop crying. He was a very loud crier!!!

Miracles continue. We just need to learn to see them for what they are. For example, during the span of 18 months, I was in 3 separate car accidents, none of which was my fault, and in 2 of which my car was totaled. Yet, I escaped basically unscathed. A miracle.

The fact that I met a man who also went through a divorce, with very similar circumstances to the one I went through, also has 3 children, who understands where I am coming from, and understands that faith and family are above everything else. Another miracle.

After I thought I was ready to retire from teaching special education having had a trying year both at home and at school, a special education job practically fell into my lap and I am loving it. Still another miracle.

My mom is the most faith-filled person I know. She lived on her faith, and showed me how to do the same. I have been through a divorce, a blending of two families (after an annulment and convalidation), and many a tough time dealing with family challenges/issues, but my faith has kept me going.

Church has been my refuge, the "quietest" place, where I can come to calm my thoughts and focus my mind on God and Jesus' steady, undying love for me, the real me, the me, with all that my heart has to offer – my joys and my sorrows, my worries and my hopes, my weaknesses and my strengths. I have discovered the beauty of Adoration, and commit myself for one hour to the Lord's presence. Here is where I find the church at its quietest, but Mass is where I can take Him in and rejoice with my spiritual family, that God is alive and well, and living in us all!

I attend Mass because I want to adore, praise and worship God and Jesus Christ, His Son, our Lord, who died for us so that we could experience perfect union with Him some day. It has taken me and continues to take a lifetime of learning how to love, and how to give of oneself, just as He did. Just as my mom did. In Jesus Christ, we have all that we need. This is my belief, my faith, and my strength.

✠

His hair shone with white radiance. The old pastor who carried me up the stairs to our church. I was three. He looked like God. The church like heaven.

So, I loved to go.

Snuggled in the pew. My Grammy, arms around. Mama cradling newborn babe. Dad and Granddad, ushers, serving.

So, I loved to go.

My friends were there. And we were teens. Worshiping together. Or giggling. Happily belonging.

So, I loved to go.

Twenty-one…content to be hand-in-hand with my Faith filled Love. Knowing Jesus. In a new True way!

So, we loved to go to Mass.

A parcel of children to worship and share with. Struggling sometimes. Learning as they did. Loving as they did.

So, we loved to go to Mass.

Community! Singing. Listening. Praying. Contemplating. Or is it daydreaming?

God brings me back. Forgives me. Grows me. Teaches me through His Word.

So, I love to go to Mass!

There in all of that. Family. Friends. Our Priest. The liturgy itself. When I participate. And He helps me, you know. The **Holy Spirit**!

I love to go to Mass!

What? Our Pastor asked me to serve? Close to Jesus in a new and precious way. My knees knocking. Each face coming. Eager to receive. **Jesus**! Cradled in my unworthy hand.

I LOVE to go to Mass!

Grace upon Grace. I travel up. HE meets me there. In Mass! Real and Radiant. To Love us. Save us. Carry me Up. Our **FATHER**!

HE is the reason **I LOVE to go to Mass!**

I am a 68-year-old "cradle Catholic." When I was in high school and college, I was undecided if I would remain with the Church. I kept going to Mass, though, partly out of habit, and partly in case I decided to remain Catholic. Thanks in large part to the comfort I found at Mass, I have remained in the Church.

The trials of my working life occasionally have led to bouts of depression, some quite severe, and the strength and comfort I found in prayer in Mass each Sunday helped me overcome them. I believe that daily Mass at the Pentagon during Lent is the main reason I made it through the most trying time in my career with my sanity intact. The support I found at Mass also allowed me to see job opportunities and act on them when I would have been too blind or afraid to otherwise try.

Now that I am comfortably retired after a satisfactory career, I go to give thanks for what God has given me, and I still find comfort for my much smaller problems.

I am a cradle Catholic and have been a parishioner at St. Mary of Sorrows since 2007. I have always been a faithful Catholic attending Mass on Sundays and Holy Days (when I didn't forget). I retired in 2015 and, at the suggestion of a friend, I started attending daily Mass. I wish I could clearly explain the difference daily Mass has made in my life, my attitude, my family and most especially in my relationship with God. I received a St. Paul Daily Missal as a gift from my wife after my retirement and started learning how to use it.

As we all know, in early 2020, the pandemic struck and we were not allowed to go to any Mass. I continued my daily routine by watching a Mass every morning. I felt thankful that

I was able to attend Mass, but I knew something was missing. Yes, I know we all had the opportunity for Spiritual Communion and that was a blessing; however, I needed more. My daughter is a parishioner at another local parish and she invited me to a Sunday communion service there. I jumped at the invitation because it was my only opportunity to actually receive Holy Communion for several months. The communion service was conducted outside the church and we all went into the church and received communion at the altar rail one by one. Unfortunately, we were required to leave immediately after receiving communion so there was no time for thankful reflection. I was so grateful, but I still had a longing for a real, in person, Mass.

Shortly thereafter, St. Mary of Sorrows began celebrating public Masses, but being over 65, I was discouraged to attend. Within a few weeks, my desire to attend and participate in the Holy Sacrifice of Mass overcame the fear that had been created and I started attending Sunday Mass. I then started attending daily Mass at another local church for a while because they had a 7:30 a.m. Mass. Once again, my attitude improved substantially and my relationship with God also returned to pre-pandemic times. In addition, during my time watching Mass, I was able to really learn how to use my St. Paul Daily Missal. I now know where all the prayers are and I am able to follow all the beautiful prayers our church has provided us in each and every daily Mass.

So, why did I come back to in-person worship? Because I just CAN'T stay away from Jesus. I NEED to be in His presence. To use an analogy I heard from Matthew Kelly, we all have a "God-sized hole" in us and try to fill it with stuff. In reality, we can only fill that hole with God.

✢

Participating in the Holy Sacrifice of the Mass, in person, has become very important to me in the past two years. I do not know how I managed to miss the open invitation to participate often…even daily!

Some background: I am a "cradle Catholic," educated in high school by the Christian Brothers, and encouraged in the Faith by my parents. But when I entered adulthood, I was enticed by the world to turn away from God. I went to Church, occasionally, and prayed fervently when life got overwhelming or challenging or scary. But I was going through the motions.

After I got married to a fine Catholic woman, we went to Church routinely on Sundays, or Saturday evenings. We "got involved" with our Parishes as we navigated my Navy career and grew a family, including at St. Mary of Sorrows Parish. We manned the booths at the Labor Day Picnic, ushered for Midnight Mass at Christmas and the Easter Vigil. Our children were involved in altar serving, children's choir, and CCD. But inside ME, I realize now that I was going through the motions…thinking I was being "a good Catholic."

Then my wife "told me" we were going to make a Pilgrimage to the Holy Land. And St Joseph-like, I was NOT going to debate the subject when it was clear the decision had been made.

My life changed forever in those nine days. We had a SUPERIOR in-country guide who introduced us to "the Fifth Gospel": the Holy Land on which our Savior Jesus Christ walked, and preached, and healed, and suffered, died and was raised from the tomb. It is important to note at this point that I had spent a year in the Holy Land, in 1976, as a military observer with the United Nations Truce Supervision Organization. I had lived in Damascus and Jerusalem for six months each. Sad to say, I COMPLETELY MISSED the opportunity presented to me then by the Holy Spirit to grow in my faith, and love for Jesus!

Our Pilgrimage director encouraged us to be open to an "Ah-ha moment." Mine came on Mount Tabor at the Church of the Transfiguration - on Ash Wednesday - when I had the incredible realization that though we were reminded that "we are dust" it is through Jesus that we have the opportunity to join Him in eternal glory - if only we will turn away from the world and embrace Jesus, and his commandment to Love.

We arrived home in Northern Virginia in March, 2020. The following Monday we began the two-week lockdown to flatten the curve. Suddenly we were cut off from Mass, in any form! We craved direction and opportunity to continue our growth in the Faith that had been sparked in the Holy Land. Thankfully, our parish priests figured out how to share their private daily Masses over the Internet. As small groups were allowed to participate in Adoration, even though participation at Mass was not yet permitted, we found ways to pray, adore and grow closer to the Trinity. Today, when I am unable to attend Mass for whatever reason, my day feels incomplete. I have grown in my faith, depend on the Trinity more than I could ever have imagined, and have a particular love for Mary of the Seven Sorrows and St. Joseph. I believe God used the pandemic to focus my attention on Him. It was truly provi-dence that brought me to St. Mary of Sorrows Church so many years ago, especially now that we have a beautiful Church with spectacular stained-glass depictions of our Patron's Sorrows.

THE QUIET. I LOVE THE QUIET OF THE CHURCH EARLY IN THE morning, or in the middle of the day, or in the evening. I love the quiet for Eucharistic Adoration. I love that I can bring my pain, my doubts, my weakness, my scars and I am more than accepted, I am welcomed. If I am at peace, that peace grows in the presence of Our Lord. Goodness fills the air in our beautiful church. The music. The communal prayer. I love hearing the voices of many coming together. If I am at peace, if I am in awe, then joining my voice to so many others at Mass, during Holy Hour, is exhilarating, a source of joy. If I am troubled, if I am lonely, then it gives me a path to solace and community. The music and the prayers remind me that I am not alone. Ever.

The other day I received some difficult personal news while I was at work. My colleagues responded with kindness, but it was a tough day. On my way home from work, I knew that I could go into the church and find Our Lord and His gentleness and His incredible love for me in everything. And so, I spent some time with Him, just sitting, just absorbing what He offered. When I left, I was still weak, I was still scarred, but I also was quietly peaceful and stronger.

This is all new for me. Although I am a "cradle Catholic," it was not until a couple of years ago that I began to notice a change, that I came to see, came to understand, that His Love was for me too. As ground was broken for our new church, my faith began to break open. As the church rose from the ground, my faith grew. As we dedicated our church for the glory of God, I was blessed to be able to dedicate myself to Him as well.

Is it perfect? No. The building, as beautiful as it is, is imperfect. We are certainly not perfect. My faith, your faith, is not expressed perfectly, but given the opportunity, it will come closer and closer each day as we try to be open to what He calls us to be.

Why do I go to Mass? Because it is where I find Him most completely. Why do I want others to come? So that they too can share in this wonder in whatever way their heart leads, so they too have the opportunity to bask in His love and thus become more able to lead others to Him as well.

LIKE MANY CRADLE CATHOLICS, MY PARENTS BROUGHT MY brother and me to Mass every week. No matter what. When we went on vacation, my brother and I would say, "Aren't we taking a vacation from going to church also?" Of course, the answer would be "no." We don't take a vacation from Jesus. We would also stay for the whole Mass. We didn't leave until the last note of the last song was played. That was the end of Mass and we didn't leave until then.

As I grew up and went off to college, I had a choice. Do I keep going to Mass? It actually wasn't much of a choice. I knew that is what I had to do, what I needed to do. But as I grew deeper in my faith, I began to understand the Mass more, understand why my parents brought me every week. There was meaning in the Mass. Without our faith and the Mass, where was the meaning to life? What was the point of living, working, struggling, suffering, without the Mass (and Jesus) to show us and give us purpose?

I developed a habit of going to daily Mass when I could. This further strengthened my love and appreciation for the Mass and Eucharist in my life. It provided a foundation for my day. A rock and stronghold for my life, as the psalmist says. Now I try to go to Mass every day. It guides my day as the true meaning for my life is presented to me every day. When I miss daily Mass, there is something lost that day. The day is not as full and my focus on the important parts of life are not as sharp.

Now that I have a family, we go to Mass every Sunday with no exceptions. When we are on vacation, we go to Mass. When we are camping in the middle of nowhere in upstate New York, we bathe in an outdoor shower or the river, drive 30 minutes and go to Mass. We don't take a vacation from Jesus, and Jesus doesn't take a vacation from us. The Mass is there to remind us every week (or every day) where our meaning and purpose comes from.

Peace

"Peace I leave with you; my peace I give to you."

— JOHN 14:27

As a kid, Mass was something I was just used to doing. We went every Sunday at our local parish and faithfully attended religious education classes. I understood that Mass was something important because we were never allowed to let a social event like a birthday party or sleepover get in the way of it.

Fast forward to the summer after my junior year of high school when I helped run a weeklong retreat for freshmen and sophomores. This retreat showed me the power of relying on God through a daily routine of prayer and reception of the sacraments. There was a tangible peace that I experienced at the end of Mass each morning. I just wanted to be able to stay and rest in that sunlit chapel all day.

At this same retreat, a college student volunteer shared his witness which included his encounter with the Eucharist. He invited retreatants to come speak with him if they had any questions. I had never heard someone speak about the Eucharist with such conviction and love, so I had to know more! He explained the beauty of every Mass—that Jesus is truly present, Heaven meets Earth, and the angels and saints are present with us. He handed me his copy of "The Lamb's Supper" by Scott Hahn and told me to keep it, with the caveat that I must hand it on to someone else to read when I finished it.

During my senior year of high school, I slowly began reading "The Lamb's Supper." The author, Dr. Scott Hahn, is a convert to the faith, and eloquently walks his readers through the Old Testament connections to the Eucharist as well as the "why" behind the prayers and gestures we repeat at every Mass. This book helped me fall in love with Mass. I remember walking through the hallways of my public school between classes and just being floored by the beauty, truth, and goodness that I was becoming convicted of as I read about the Mass. I would highly recommend this book!

The experience of a daily routine of prayer, the witness of a friend, and the writings of Dr. Scott Hahn helped cultivate a desire within my heart to attend Mass as often as possible— even daily when I could!

Since high school, attending Mass has been a highlight of my week, and draws me deeper into a personal relationship with Jesus. On the days when I don't receive Jesus in the Eucharist, I notice a tangible difference in the way I love the Lord, others, and myself. The grace that is received at Mass is real! Hearing the Word of God has brought me conviction, courage, hope, peace, and reassurance. Bringing my sufferings, joys, hopes, desires, and dreams to the altar for Jesus to transform, just as He transforms the bread and wine into His Body and Blood, has been humbling. It reminds me that I am not the Savior. He is God and I am not. Being a part of the Body of Christ and praying in union with the angels and saints reminds me I am a part of a faith which is much bigger than I am. Praying the Creed gives me strength as I recall the martyrs of the Church who have died for the truth of the words we dare to proclaim in prayer each week. Even struggling to overcome the distraction of a cute baby or the food I'll eat after Mass, has been a beautiful and challenging opportunity to refocus my attention on God and His love which I hunger for more than anything else.

The Mass is far more to me than my Sunday duty or a box to be checked off. It is the place where all of the desires of my heart are met. It is, as the Catechism of the Catholic Church says, "the source and the summit" (CCC 1324) of my day and my life as a Christian. It is Jesus given to me so that I may be a living tabernacle to be sent out to share the Good News with others.

THE HOLY MASS IS GUARANTEED THE BEST PART OF MY DAY. It is a piece of Heaven brought into creation, and God's sacrifice of His Only Son gives me clarity of mind and purpose.

When I wake, I am not sure what the day will bring or if I am doing God's will, but by going to Mass *I know* that I am doing the right thing. And this Holy Sacrifice recasts my day like nothing else in this world.

Just like the bread and wine are changed into our Lord but still have the appearances of bread and wine, I hope that I am being changed to be more like our Lord and Savior little by little, even though I am outwardly not any different.

The Holy Mass also protects me from spiritual dangers. I am more equipped to interact with difficult people or situations after attending Mass and interacting with other members of the Body of Christ. I can hear that inner voice of Christ more clearly when my day includes the Mass. It is as if the static and background noises of my thoughts are tuned out and I can think more clearly and have peace.

The Holy Mass also gives me the opportunity to pray for myself and others in a more efficacious way than during my normal busy day. I know my spiritual life is in order when I go to Mass and then I know that I can pray for my family and others.

I pray for those who do not understand the peace and joy of the Mass. They are suffering like me and are looking in all directions for peace. May they be brought closer to Jesus and His Holy Church by discovering the Holy Mass!

I HAVE A FRIEND AND COWORKER WHO DID NOT LIKE TO travel on weekends because she did not want to miss church services at the Christian church she attended. I naively asked her why she didn't just seek another church in the local community to attend when she was out of town, and she replied that it was uncomfortable because the services were not the same.

Having spent decades in the military and my current job traveling across the country and the world, I took for granted that while there may be very subtle differences in the Mass services from church-to-church or diocese-to-diocese, our Roman Catholic faith is truly that: Catholic = Universal.

WHY I GO TO MASS:

- To receive the Body of Christ;
- To hear the Word of God, as well as the homily of the priests and deacons, inspired by the Holy Spirit;

- To witness the transubstantiation of the bread and wine into the body and blood of Christ;
- To pray in communion with others who share our Catholic faith;
- To separate myself from other worldly distractions and reflect upon God's word and how it pertains to me;
- To petition God, not only for my own intentions, but also in support of others' prayers and needs;
- The Penitential Act allows me to deliberately pause and reflect upon my sins and shortcomings and ask God's forgiveness and assistance in righting my path;
- To enjoy the fellowship of singing the hymns with other parishioners and the choir, and the additional means of prayer these hymns provide;
- To be an example for my family, friends and community;
- To share in the sacraments, rites and tradition of a faith that has been passed on to us by the Church for two millennia.

I GO TO MASS IN THANKFULNESS. THANKFULNESS FOR A multitude of blessings so freely, generously, and astonishingly given. Thankfulness for life itself - rich in triumphs and defeats, rewards and punishments, sorrows and joys - life as it is lived. Thankful, too, for the grace given to pass the trials of faith, hope, and love crafted to test and increase my devotion. Thankful for forgiveness for the times I turned away from the true and the beautiful, times that were empty and barren, times "I fled Him down the nights and down the days" (Francis Thompson's poem "The Hound of Heaven"), as a willing victim of my own willfulness.

I go to Mass because it sustains the faith that sustains me. Sunday without Mass is incomplete, missing an essential quality that is difficult to express but no less real. How modest an obligation and how wondrously rewarding: the Body and Blood, Soul and Divinity of the Son of God await us.

I go to Mass aspiring for that day when I hear the words "Pray, brethren, that my sacrifice and yours may be acceptable to God, the almighty Father," and know for once that my thoughts, attention, and devotion have been as entire, complete, and as perfect as my imperfection can render.

I go to Mass in awe. Awe that among the countless multitude of souls willed into existence, God chose to create me to live this life and live for all endless time with Him in Heaven if I but choose to love Him. I love God, I love the life He gave me, and I love the Mass. I go to Mass out of love.

BASICALLY, I GO TO MASS BECAUSE IT IS A SAFE SANCTUARY where I can truly be myself. Receiving Jesus and being in His Presence gives me strength to go on living through the daily grind with little to no regular spiritual interaction with other believers. We live far away from family who are practicing Catholics and it can feel at times quite lonely. There are many demands placed on families, parents, and individuals these days, and even with the best intentions, it is easy to become overwhelmed by what the world demands of you, and daunting to try to cut through all the entangling and competing pressures on your own. It is important to me to raise our two daughters to love Jesus and to depend on Him, because we do not have strong faith ties outside of the home anymore in our family to help with this communal task, and this causes me great sadness when I stop to think about it sometimes. However, I take courage that although it may seem a herculean and maybe even futile task with me leading it, nothing is impossible for God.

On a more personal note, I really like that God usually gives me encouraging little surprises through the other people I see at Mass. This could be the joy of hearing someone putting his whole heart into singing, or looking into the eyes of the Eucharistic Minister as I receive Jesus. I like to imagine that all these people lining up for communion are part of my heavenly family, that they also must love God very much, and I might see them in Heaven one day even if the path here on earth is not full of a great deal of spiritual companionship. This brings me a lot of joy. I feel I do not have to be anything different from "just myself" here, and that I have permission to bask in His Holy Love and Presence after receiving Him. I do not have to answer to anyone else during this time, and it is okay to remove my masks of other worldly identities for a brief moment, undisturbed.

I GO TO MASS BECAUSE I AM DRAWN TO IT: JESUS IS THERE, waiting. At Mass I find peace. At every Mass Jesus comes in a special way when at the consecration of the bread and wine the miracle of the real presence of Jesus takes place. Only in the Eucharist is Jesus truly present Body, Blood, Soul and Divinity. At communion we receive Jesus completely.

After communion is, for me, the best time to talk to Jesus or just listen. He is physically closest to me then: really and truly present. It is comforting to know that He strengthens and sanctifies me. He heals and forgives me.

Like Padre Pio I ask Jesus to stay with me to be with me throughout the day.

I WENT TO MASS FOR YEARS…DECADES…BECAUSE IT WAS expected, but when traveling, I didn't feel any compulsion to go out of my way to find a Mass. Who would know anyway?

I was involved, but only in a cursory way. It was all skin-deep. That is no longer.

Now I go because I need to…want to…long to.

Sometimes I go because I am feeling confident in my relationship with God. I go to celebrate. To thank. To adore.

But there are other times when I am uncertain… or confused… or even afraid. Why go then? Because in my heart… in the hidden corners…I know that those days are the days when I need to go the most. I may not walk out of Mass any surer, with any answers, or calm and peaceful, but I walk out knowing it was good and right that I was there, that going on those days is part of the process of growing closer to Him.

I am learning that He can handle my bad days… and handle them better than I do.

God has waited, and continues to wait, patiently for me to allow myself to hear His whisper call my name. He has not pushed or shouted or caused lightning and thunder to get my attention.

Like the child I am, He has spoken to me in kind, gentle tones, with soothing words. Always there, even when I could not believe He wanted me. Me.

I would like to say that I no longer get confused or frightened, but that would not be so. But each time… each time I go back… each time I hear the words… they become a bit clearer. Each time I receive Him my heart grows closer to His.

I go to Mass because I want to know I am loved. I go to Mass because I am falling love with the One who loves me above all else.

✟

THE REASONS I ATTEND MASS ARE, AS A POOR SINNER, TO GIVE thanks to God and to find meaning and purpose in this life while encountering Jesus Christ through scripture, the homily, and the Holy Eucharist. I yearn to grasp a deeper understanding of the Truth to gain the confidence and spiritual strength to face the challenges of life and share the Gospel with doubters and unbelievers.

Worshiping God in a faith-filled community brings a sense of peace and happiness leading to a desire to serve the Lord and others. Striving to follow in the footsteps of Christ, although I stumble frequently, helps provide me with clarity of thought leading to virtuous action in word and deed that I hope is pleasing to God the Father.

THE REASON THAT I GO TO MASS IS VERY SIMPLE. I NEED GOD. I just can't do it alone.

I think it is a common misconception that people who go to Mass are there because they are holier than others; for most of us the opposite is true. I attend Mass on Sundays because I struggle in many ways. I worry all the time about myself, my family members, the country, and the world and I come to Mass to ask God to take those worries and fears from me. In my mind, I imagine that I am placing my fears in front of the altar. Laying them at the foot of the cross allows me to put it all in God's hands. When I receive the Eucharist, I feel close to Jesus and in the moments after, I know that it is a special time when He is most alive in me and I can ask Him for whatever I need. I will admit that there are times when I am at Mass and I find my mind wandering and need to pull my attention back. However, I try not to worry about that or feel guilty because I know God knows that I am trying.

I have never regretted *going* to Mass, but I do regret it if I *don't* go. When I am walking out of the church at the end of

Mass, I know that God is with me, and I don't ever have to do anything alone.

WHO WOULD NOT WANT TO VISIT THEIR MOST TREASURED friend? For me, attending Mass is like visiting my very best friend. My Lord, God, is the best of sympathetic listeners as I strive to unite myself as closely as possible with Him and through Him in preparation of offering myself totally to Him.

He is all knowing, non-judgmental, and accepts me as I am. He quiets my anxious heart. He enriches my soul. His peace, connection and deep feeling of contentment envelops me as I prepare for the greatest of celebrations: the Mass.

No matter how frenzied life is, coming to the table of the Lord, striving to renew my baptismal promises and fulfilling the will of God is a constant in my life. It is so comforting knowing that I am being embraced in His love.

I bask in awe at the pageantry and liturgical traditions: the grand procession of the priest, the liturgy of the Word with its application to my life and to my salvation and to the liturgy of the Eucharist, the supreme sacrifice of Our Redeemer, where I can offer myself up with all earnestness and concentration to the Lord God.

This is why I go to Mass. This is what attendance at Mass means to me: the greatest gift ever!

I GO TO MASS TO FIND PEACE AND COMFORT AND LOVE FROM the one who loves me perfectly. Even though I am not worthy of God's love, I cannot live without it. I am truly humbled by God's greatness and His love for each of us. I struggle with holiness and fall short, but I want to grow in faith. Sometimes I cannot imagine God's love for me and am humbled by the goodness He brings into my life. He has surrounded me with opportunities and blessings and people to help me grow in faith and love.

When I attend Mass, I am nourished by His Word, as I understand it. Then the priest explains His Word, which always brings clarity and insight to my understanding. I am then nourished by His Body. Once I have been filled with His love, I go out into the world to be His light and help others to know and love Him through my kindness and caring. I don't always do a great job, so I humbly return to God for His forgiveness and love. If I approach Him with my heart open, He is there to nourish.

Mass is a time for reflection and offerings to God. I am reminded of His mercy and all that He has done for all of us. He died so we can live. I want us all to know and embrace His love, so in Heaven we can be with Him, truly satisfied and finally at peace.

WHY I GO TO MASS.

Because it is all true!

I started a journey back to God 30 years ago.

I tried it my way. It did not work out. It all started falling apart. I needed to know what it was all about. I could no longer go on. I needed real answers. I asked Jesus to help me and to show me the way. Jesus showed up. I knew He was there. He helped me get back on track. He helps me stay on track. Many left me. Jesus never did. Jesus sent me others. I pray He will never let me go.

Jesus died for all those sins I committed. Jesus died for all those people I had hurt. Jesus died so that I could have a second chance. Jesus helped me clean up the mess. I am forever grateful.

I am grateful for the peace Jesus has provided that surpasses all understanding.

I am grateful to know that the Blessed Mother, saints, Jesus, angels, and Father hear my every prayer and that my prayers are always answered just as they should be.

I want to know Jesus. I want to know my Blessed Mother. I want to know the Father. I want to know the Holy Spirit. I want to listen to them and move where they want me to go. I need their love. They never fail to give.

I want to be in communion with Jesus and receive Him in the Most Blessed sacrament. I want to offer my thanksgiving and gratitude to the Father and Son. I need the Holy Spirit to breathe for me, to live in me, to help me to love. I need the Blessed Mother to nurture me. I need the Father to discipline me. I need Jesus to be my friend.

I want to love God the way He deserves to be loved. I want to help others and learn how to love them, even the most difficult.

I want to become the person God created me to be.

I want to bear witness to my Lord.

I want to feel joy in my heart.

I want to remain in the state of grace.

I want my lantern lit when Jesus comes again, and I do not want to run out of oil.

I want to worship the Creator, the all loving, all good, all merciful, compassionate God.

For all these things, and so many, many more, I go to Mass.

As soon as I enter through the door, I come into a very sacred space and feel uncluttered by the world outside. I know I have just entered into the celestial place that I am journeying toward. The lighted candles and vestments and the beautiful altar bring about a heavenly presence, where I confess to God my sins, and where I hear His empowering and life-giving Word that brings me so alive and deeper into God and my faith.

The homily inspires me, as the priest reflects on the meaning of the Word, especially when he tells us of the saint of the day. The Prayers of the Faithful remind me of the needs of our world for which I pray. Part 2 of the liturgy brings forth from me remembrance and thanksgiving for Christ's sacrifice. The sign of peace, when I raise my hand toward my friends who are in fellowship with me in the Lord, brings to me a joy that the world cannot offer.

By attending Mass, not only am I fed HIS WORD — Christ feeds me with HIMSELF. All in attendance now have Christ running through their veins. I am deeply with Him and the others in the congregation. What peace, what joy, what presence I feel. I am full. The blessing at the end of Mass gives me the grace to be more Christ-like and to go forth to spread the news of the Kingdom to others, especially by my actions.

I ask myself, why others do not experience the Mass more often. I am elated by the presence of the Lord, inspired by His Word, and by the fellowship of those who attend each time I attend Mass. Are others too blinded by the clutter of the world to see what is afforded to us when we attend the Holy Sacrifice of the Mass? I wouldn't miss it for the world!!

I LOVE GOING TO THE MASS BECAUSE OF THE EUCHARIST. After receiving Holy Communion, after most people leave the Church, I feel the presence of Jesus in my heart. I really do not talk with Him directly. I just sit and reflect on whatever comes to mind. I listen to get a better understanding of what is really the issue behind the situation. I know it is our Lord guiding my thoughts for I arrive at a place of hope and peace, and then Jesus usually has some action for me to take.

Our church is beautiful, and I live to come to this oasis. I love its simple grandeur, and the predominance of white and light are joy inspiring. The music program is also so lovely.

I GO TO MASS BECAUSE GOD LOVES ME,
and I love Him.
I go because He beckons
with love,
with mercy.
I go because I need His help,
His peace,
His grace,
His strength.
I go because He is the one constant
through all the changes in my life,
and all the changes in this crazy world.
Even when I was not faithful to Him,
He remained faithful and waiting for me.
I go because He is the way, the truth, the life;
The source of everything holy and good;
The uncreated creator;
my Lord;
my Savior.
I go because when I called out to Him,
He showed up in a huge way with
His love,
His mercy.
I go because He beckons.
I go because God loves me,
and I love Him.

Regardless of how "crazy" things might seem to be all around us, my faith, my beliefs have convinced me God has "time" to listen to me, to help me sort through all the background noise of life these days, and help me focus on what's important. Going to Mass helps me know, in a special way, that God still listens. In Mass I can literally look at God, under the appearance of bread and wine, and know that I am talking not to some ethereal spirit, but a living breathing person. One who might have walked this Earth 2,000 years before me, but a living breathing, physically PRESENT person. He lets me – or any of us – tell Him what's bothering me, or to let me thank Him for that for which I am grateful (which is everything), and His listening helps to keep me on track.

Given the normal rhythm of life, I think we always have a lot to pray about/pray for; I know I do! However, the past 18 months or so have added another layer of prayer topics: the whole COVID-19 pandemic; it's effect on the health and well-being of our family and friends; how it's impacting, in particular, the small businesses owned by friends, etc. Add to that the highly polarized environment surrounding seemingly ANY topic these days, and anyone would have a lot to pray about!

Now, while I love the joy of communal worship via the Mass, I also find a great deal of solace and joy in private prayer. One of my favorite New Testament quotes is Matthew 6:6, "But when you pray, go to your inner room, close the door, and pray to your Father in secret. And your Father who sees in secret will repay you." So, one of the ways I've been dealing with all of this is an increase in my private prayer. It's refreshing and reinvigorating, spiritually, emotionally, and physically to set some time aside, go to my "prayer chair" and sit and say my prayers. I have a regular set of prayers I like to recite, but the intentions vary from day-to-day. I look at it as my time with Jesus, my time with God, and that is MOST encouraging.

Mass and private prayer: one plus one equals a WHOLE lot more!

WHEN MY FAITH IS STRONG, I GET GREAT PEACE FROM MASS.

When my faith is weak as Mother Teresa also admitted, "I know that the closer I get to the person I believe God wants me to be, the happier I am."

I DID NOT REALIZE HOW MUCH I NEEDED "CHURCH" UNTIL THE pandemic arose. Although I usually only went on Sundays, its absence was really isolating to me. It was before everything was live- streamed.

When I realized how dry my faith had become, I decided not only to go to church on Sundays, but as much as I can during the week as well.

I have come to know that the faith which sustains me doesn't just come from myself, but when I am in fellowship with others, and my faith needs constant nurturing, I cannot spend enough time in worship. I understand that my need for a relationship with God comes from the fact that I know what it is like to be without Him! Not that He needs me so much as I need Him. I cannot exist without this gift, and I want him to know and understand that this (gift) is something I want to share with others!

I WAS BORN CATHOLIC AND GOING TO MASS ON SUNDAY WAS what we did. I went to Catholic school, my friends who went to public school (we called them "publics") didn't. So, Catholics go to Mass; "publics" didn't. That's just the way it was.

When I got older, I met a boy. He was being sent to Vietnam. I had heard that the life expectancy of a lieutenant in the infantry wasn't very good. I don't know why someone would tell me that but they did. So, I decided I needed to do something to help the odds a bit. Pray certainly, but maybe going to Mass every day before school would help. So, every day I offered my Mass and communion up for his safe return. When he returned after that year without a scratch, I thought I better go for another year in thanksgiving.

Just as I thought I might be able to sleep in a bit, the U.S. Army, in its infinite wisdom, decided to send him back again. To make a long story short, we have been married for 50 years. What I learned was that going to Mass was not just something Catholics did or a way to even the odds. I learned that the holy sacrifice of the Mass is my strength, my comfort, and my privilege.

WHY DO I GO TO MASS? TO:

Be with Jesus Christ, my Lord and Savior, my Friend, my Comforter, my Provider, my Miracle Worker, my Deliverer, my Beloved.

Praise and Worship Jesus to thank Him for His Sacrifice of Love on the Cross for me, for the forgiveness of my sins.

Bring to Jesus the gifts of my love, prayers, daily work, joys, and sufferings, offering these gifts for the salvation of souls, reparation for sins, the reunion of all Christians, and for the intentions of the Holy Father. Pope Paul VI said, "The Holy Mass is the most perfect form of prayer." I am learning that when I unite my offerings with the Holy Sacrifice of the

Mass, they can and will bear fruit – in my life and the lives of others.

Receive Jesus Christ in the Holy Eucharist. I am in awe of the miracle that takes place at each and every Mass when the priest – who stands in the person of Jesus Christ and through the power of the Holy Spirit – changes simple bread and wine into the Body and Blood of Jesus Christ. Jesus is my Daily Bread for my journey to Heaven. I need his love and strength each day.

Experience the love of Jesus; to be filled with His peace, love, and joy; to receive what Jesus wants to show me through the Holy Mass; and then to share with others the grace and blessings I've received from Jesus.

Glorify God. When I begin my day with Mass, my whole day goes better. St. Peter Julian Eymard said, "Hear Mass daily; it will prosper the whole day. All your duties will be performed the better for it, and your soul will be stronger to bear its daily cross. The Mass is the most holy act of religion; you can do nothing that can give greater glory to God or be more profitable for your soul than to hear Mass both frequently and devoutly."

Pray for my family; the holy souls in purgatory; our Church and its leaders; our world and its leaders; those who are sick, suffering, dying; those who don't know Jesus; and those who have walked away from Him.

Receive the Lord's grace (unmerited favor); to be strengthened against sin; to grow in virtue; to be transformed into who God made me to be; and to reach Heaven – where we will be united in love forever with God the Father, God the Son, and God the Holy Spirit, all the angels and saints, and our family and friends for all eternity.

✠

I RECOMMEND GOING TO MASS TO OTHERS BECAUSE GOD wants us to; we need to talk to God and it gives us graces. God in the commandments told us to respect the Sabbath day, and the Church tells us to do this by going to Mass. Therefore, you should go to Mass out of obedience to Him.

Also, we should go to Mass to see God. God is present at the Mass, and the best way to strengthen a relationship with someone is to spend time with that person. Therefore, going to Mass strengthens our relationship with God.

Thirdly, Mass gives us sacramental graces to help us reach Heaven, the goal of humanity.

I GO TO MASS (SOMETIMES DAILY) BECAUSE SOMETHING INSIDE me (my soul) craves it.

I like to start my day going to Mass.

I feel at peace and centered when I go to Mass.

This world is so hectic that I need the centering presence of Christ. I know I can get this anywhere I am since Christ is in me, but going to Mass seems to center me more due to the quiet. I always search out churches wherever I go (I travel frequently). I can learn a lot about the local community by attending Mass.

MY PERCEPTION AND FEELINGS ABOUT MASS CAME ONLY AFTER I changed my attitude about seeking a relationship with Christ. I remember going to Mass since I was little. Then as I got older, I stopped going to Mass, because I was not getting anything from Mass. For decades I felt nothing when attending Mass, rather it was just another Sunday at church. When I started attending Bible studies, reading God's word and spiritual writings, I started to get to know more of who

God is, and how much God loves His creation, us, and me. I started to believe with my mind and heart that God is infinite mercy, love, and blessings. I began to see attending Mass as visiting Christ and all Heaven. When I sought a relationship with Christ and strived to be committed to attending Mass, my eyes of faith increased. I began to see and to believe the Eucharist IS the Body and Blood of Christ.

As my eyes of faith have increased, I realized the great richness and treasure in the Mass is present and alive at each Mass. I started to see Mass as a personal encounter with Christ and other persons of the Trinity. I went from getting nothing from Mass to knowing that when attending Mass, God would be speaking to me in some form. To me this was a long process, because of my own lack of seeking and commitment. It boils down to fostering a relationship with Christ; thus, I must give myself to Christ as Christ gives Himself to me; and Christ means what He says.

As my relationship with Christ grew, the more I wanted to attend Mass. The more I attended Mass, the more I had peace in the midst of my storms. I know this is from God, because if I could have created this peace I was seeking, I would have done so a long time ago. Although God is everywhere, I believe by participating in the Mass eventually God transforms the person's faith into seeing things "the God way."

At this point, I am patiently waiting on the Lord to show me more of the mystery of the Mass, and I know He will. Mass is not a time, as God transcends time and space, and for God everything is present. So, every time I attend Mass, I see more and more how much God loves me and how much He wants to bless me. When I feel hurt, am bothered, or overwhelmed with life, I know Christ is saying give Me your hurts and burdens, so He can replace them with His joy and peace that will fill my interior.

I lived decades without knowing and living this, through my own actions. "God is Love" is not just a slogan to be placed on a coffee cup. He is loving, and his generosity is so great that He cannot be outdone, and all I had to do was accept it. It is my belief, by attending Mass frequently, the more Christ's love and ways become alive; and, through such encounters time and time again, there is no way one can remain the same. It is interior peace and joy to see Christ in others and that Christ's love will become one's way.

Oddly, I now realize not attending Mass for so many years did, eventually, show me that attending Mass gives life a vibrancy and interior peace and joy that cannot be gained from worldly ways. I never want to make Mass unimportant ever again, because I believe there is no way when time is given to God with one's heart and soul by participating in the Mass that a person ends up empty; rather, the eyes of faith increase and the treasure and richness that enter one's interior life are more than one could imagine. I know things are revealed/become apparent in God's perfect timing; so, I will be committed to attending Mass and never want to have Mass dryness ever again.

Today, I now realized I stopped attending Mass because I did not have a friendship/relationship with Christ. Like with personal relationships, there must be investment and commitment for the relationship to be strong and fruitful. We human beings are in constant search for more than what we have, for things to make us happy, but nothing will compare to knowing and relying on God. His love and peace truly cannot be found anywhere on this earth, except through Jesus Christ and the Mass, and, sadly, for many, cannot even be described.

I ATTEND MASS EVERY WEEK TO ENCOUNTER LOVE, TO experience Peace, and to witness a Miracle. As I have learned from my spiritual journey, God is Love – His very being is Love, through and through. I dearly love my wife, my children (all grown now), and I look forward to someday loving grand-children. Although my parents are no longer living, I still deeply love them, too. As deeply as I feel this love for my family, it is incomparable to the love that God has for us. This seems too hard to understand – so I keep trying. The more I encounter God, the more I am able to draw comparisons and analogies to my life and the world I experience. For example, before becoming a parent, I simply didn't understand the depths of parental love. Loving like a parent is one window into better understanding God's Love for us. Then there is the Crucifix that welcomes us every time we approach the altar – that also reminds us of His love for us, and I am still reminded that I have more to learn, more to grow, and more to encounter.

I experience Peace at Mass. I am with my brothers and sisters in Christ. We are worshiping our loving Father, Son, and Holy Spirit – together. Outside the Mass there are almost certainly many things we don't agree upon, but at the Mass, we can commune in Peace that our Triune God has created us, sustains us, and has a plan for each of us. Mass is time that we can soak in our Lord's Love, pray for guidance, and let go of the world outside, if only for a brief time. I can't count the number of times that I have entered Mass with troubles on my mind, an irritable disposition, or otherwise weighed down, but at the end of every Mass – my heart and my load are lighter and I am more at Peace.

The summit of every Mass is the Eucharist – and this is the most wonderful miracle to witness. I have witnessed many wonderful things that I have described as miraculous – the birth of my children, the smile of my wife at our wedding, the beauty of sunsets over the lake. To be sure, God was in all of these things. However, what we witness at Mass is our God using His power of creation to become physically present to us. He is not only present to us as we watch, but He is simulta-neously physically present at the actual Last Supper, and every

Mass ever held - past, present, and future. We get to witness and participate in a miracle that transcends space and time, so we get to participate in the same, one sacrifice that our Lord Jesus made two thousand years ago. I believe that Creation itself is the only miracle that compares, but we are able, in fact invited, to witness the miracle of the Eucharist every day!

There are other reasons that I enjoy Mass as well, to include the fellowship with friends and family, the beauty of the church, and of course I love music. However, it is Love, Peace and Miracles that keeps me faithfully attending Mass every week.

I HAVEN'T GIVEN A LOT OF THOUGHT OF WHY I GO TO MASS because it just feels so natural. Naturally, because it makes me feel so at ease. I feel closer to God. I feel the tug of the Lord to be nearer to Him and His church.

As a flawed individual, I know I will never be perfect, but going to Mass allows me to feel like I'm trying to be a better person - attempting to be closer to our God. Going to Mass allows me to completely dedicate a few minutes each week to pray for my deceased parents and in-laws, kids, grandkids, siblings, nephews and nieces and their families, my wife and myself. I know I can do that anytime, anywhere. But it just feels so right to pray for them at Mass. It gives me solace.

Going to Mass gives me time to listen to homilies and to step back from the craziness of today's world and reflect on what is truly important in life. Doing that also lets me see how I measure up and where I am missing the mark. And how to do better.

I truly enjoy the church community. I really enjoy seeing my fellow parishioners each week. I love seeing families as they mature and change. There is a warmth to the church family.

I go to Mass because I feel that it makes me a better person – far from perfect – but better, nonetheless.

THE ANSWER FOR ME OF WHY I GO TO MASS ISN'T EASY. I GO to learn, to visit with God. Those are the easy answers. The harder one takes an effort on my part. There is an energy in church especially when it is full of people. If you concentrate, you can feel it. The peace of it. I'm not a good writer nor do I easily believe in things, but this is different. You can truly feel it. Now that is why I go.

For me the better question is why I don't go. Fear! COVID! Busy! Will God take His time for me? God answers with…vaccines…booster…sanitizer…masks…good habits… It reminds me of a joke that I once heard. A very religious man was in a boat that capsized. He prayed with all he had and a piece of wood floated by. He ignored it and kept praying. Then came a life jacket, a buoy, more floating debris and still the result was the same. He kept praying. A boat came and he waved them off. Finally, he was too weak and called out to God and asked, "Why?" God said, "I sent you help, why didn't you make use of it?" (I like to think the boat came back and grabbed him anyhow).

So, when I ask myself, "why not?" I just don't have a good enough answer, given everything He has done to protect me!

ST. MARY OF SORROWS PARISHIONER:

I go to church because I want to give thanks to God for many things— first of all, that I'm alive. Being born three months premature, my parents didn't know whether I would survive. I'm here walking this earth 42 years later. I thank the Lord for the many gifts and talents with which He has blessed me— that I can proclaim His word, sing His praises, and share His gifts to the ends of the earth. I'm grateful to God for the gift of the rosary which we pray before Mass. I believe with this devotion wars will end, peace will return, and in heaven the angels will rejoice. I go to Mass because I want to give glory to God in the Holy Eucharist. I believe that Jesus is present in body, blood, soul and divinity in the tabernacle. I wish to show reverence to the Holy Eucharist every time I go into church.

Since childhood, my faith and attendance at Mass have been very important to me. This is why I go to church.

SHRINE OF THE SACRED HEART PARISHIONER (DC), fiancée of St. Mary of Sorrows Parishioner:

I go to Mass because I believe it's the best way to worship God in community. There is a song that says "We are Family." I think those words are very true. People come from all walks of life with different experiences, but we are united in Christ, the many parts of His one body. This is a powerful reality that I experience every time I go to church.

My parents prayed fervently and after trials were able to have me. Although I was born prematurely, they had faith that I would survive. God has granted me many blessings that I'm thankful for. Going to Mass is like the spiritual "gym" for my faith. I build up those muscles along with my fellow brothers and sisters so that when I go out into the world, I have a reservoir to draw from. This is why I go to church.

ST. MARY OF SORROWS PARISHIONER, MOTHER OF THE ABOVE St. Mary of Sorrows Parishioner:

I go to church to acknowledge the many, many blessings I have: to thank God for my sorrows, my joys, my family, my community and the daily gifts I receive from Him. I want to be close to Him and going to Mass makes me feel His presence in my life. I feel my church is my home where I can come home to thank Him and to complain to Him and do all other sorts things that we would do to a parent. The gift of my son is the biggest blessing I have received from God and I should thank Him every day for that biggest blessing.

HUSBAND OF THE ABOVE ST. MARY OF SORROWS parishioner:

I go to church because I always find comfort and feel whole, especially when I receive Him in the Eucharist. Although I know God is always around and everywhere, I have more strength to share my sorrows, joys, and appreciation in His presence and for His unending love for me. I always feel more revived when I get out of church.

WHY DO I GO TO MASS? IT'S ALL ABOUT LOVE. GOD LOVES me. There is nothing I can do to make Him love me more, nor anything I can do to make Him love me less. He has a passionate desire to share His love with me (and all humanity) in the context of a personal relationship. What I can do is to "try to" willingly and unconditionally love Him back with agape love. The closest analogy I can think of to this kind of love is the love shared between spouses or between parents and their children. This is sacrificial love. It focuses on what is best for the other person in the relationship and routinely requires willingly accepting sacrifice and hardship for the benefit of the other person. Building such meaningful relationships does not come easily, given our ego-centered nature. Every relationship comes with expectations on the part of each party. Given the world we live in, God's expectations are radically counter-cultural.

In spite of my deep desire to accept God's gift of unconditional love, the weaknesses of my humanity, my sinfulness and the corruption of the secular world make it virtually impossible for me to follow the plan God has laid out for my salvation on my own. I need help. Through the unmerited grace of His love, God has provided a multitude of support systems for my earthly pilgrimage. A very important element of that support comes from the church militant in the form of the parish community which provides inspiration, encouragement, and assistance while I travel through the trials of daily living.

However, for me, the greatest graces in God's treasury of support are the sacrament of Reconciliation, the Mass, and the Eucharist. It is through the sacrament of Reconciliation that I am able to get back on the path to the narrow gate. The Mass brings me together with the parish community to get and provide inspiration and encouragement and to receive the sacrament of the Eucharist. It is in the Eucharist that I am able bring Christ into my heart in the most personal and intimate way. So, it is through the Mass that I receive the most fulfilling and necessary nourishment for my daily journey with Christ to salvation.

A SECOND PERSPECTIVE:

A church goer wrote a letter to the editor of a newspaper and complained that it made no sense to go to church every Sunday. "I've gone for 30 years now," he wrote, "and in that time I have heard something like 3,000 sermons. For the life of me, I can't remember even one of them. So, I think I'm wasting my time and the pastors are wasting theirs by giving sermons at all."

This started a real controversy in the "Letters to the Editor" column, much to the delight of the editor. It went on for weeks until someone wrote this clincher:

"I've been married for 55 years now. In that time, my wife

has cooked over 40,000 meals. But for the life of me, I cannot recall the entire menu for a single one of those meals. However, I do know this: They all nourished me and gave me the strength I needed to do my work. If my wife had not given me these meals, I would be physically dead today. Likewise, if I had not gone to church for nourishment, I would be spiritually "dead"!

WHEN I WAS A YOUNG GIRL, I WENT BECAUSE I HAD TO. MY Catholic mom required us to be out the door by 8:45 a.m. every Sunday morning, properly dressed and ready for Mass. Proper dress meant church shoes, tights, and a dress. This was a form of torture for a *tomboy* like myself, but protest was futile. The only consolation was that my Methodist father would be at home preparing a delicious Sunday breakfast for us while we were at Mass and would have it waiting on the table when we came home! Alleluia! My Methodist father backed my mother 100% in our Catholic raising (and in most other decisions, incidentally). They sent us to Catholic school where I had fantastic Catholic role models. (Though my father was himself a *Methodist*, he was in fact one of the best *Catholic* role models I had growing up, in addition to my mother, because he lived an authentically virtuous life, and the two of them modeled perfectly their marital vocation. He would later "officially" become Catholic, but not until many years later, after he became a grandfather!).

In college, I found myself surrounded by people who did not share my Catholic faith. In fact, I had only one other Catholic friend who actually went to Mass. I found myself questioning many aspects of the faith. I began to read the scriptures each night, conducting "*experiments*" in my daily life to test the validity of Christ's teachings. (If it sounds weird, what can I say? I was a science major). Interestingly, I noticed that if I *tested* Christ's teachings in the *"laboratory"* of my everyday life, they really worked! (And on a very profound level!) Further, the fruits of putting them into practice were many! One particular fruit really stood out:

Peace. Peace in my heart and in my relationships. I could see that Christ offered a way of peace - as well as a compass - in a world that seemed to be growing increasingly confused, discontented, and disoriented. I began to discover that I was only at the *beginning* of my faith journey, even though I had completed many years of Catholic school! (As they say, when the student is ready, the teacher will appear.) I stood on the precipice of what I realized was the infinite ocean of the creativity and love of God. I would spend my life delving deeper, exploring and discovering the deeper truths. It would be a bold adventure, with surprising twists and turns. I would go on to observe time and time again, that what the secular world offered was lies and illusions that failed to stand up to scrutiny, failed to satisfy, and didn't bring peace.

Later I got married. We didn't plan to have children, as I was focused on having a career. Yet again, the Catholic Church had much to teach me and my husband about marriage. We will be forever indebted to the Catholic Church for showing us the beauty of being open to life! Amen! Today, I am the very thankful mother of 5 children, something that I never would have imagined in my younger days! Through this incredible vocation of motherhood, God reveals Himself in profound and unexpected ways! I often feel that the Catholic Church is the lone voice in a somewhat hostile world, standing up for this extraordinary and miraculous gift of life that is sadly so misunderstood by so many.

And this is why I go to Mass. Yep. I am still a tomboy. And, I don't wear tights. But I LOVE the faith and I recognize the TRUTH of our faith! I love our Lord Jesus Christ. I need to receive the Eucharist and be with my Catholic brothers and sisters at Mass so that we can strengthen and ENJOY each other! The pandemic afflicted many with loneliness and isolation. We can find joy and renewal again in returning to the familial celebration of Mass! Mass is a celebration, and it should feel that way. We have so much to celebrate!! Each day, I know that God gives me three tasks: to love, to forgive, and to serve.

Starting my day with Mass gives me the clarity and strength I need to see these tasks and focus more closely on them. I give thanks that I have the opportunity to be a part of St. Mary of Sorrows where we are truly blessed with holy and devoted priests who serve us with great fervor and devotion, bringing us closer to Jesus each and everyday! May God continue to bless each of them and this very special parish! Amen.

I THINK NOTHING PLEASES GOD MORE THAN SEEING HIS children coming humbly together to give thanks, pray, ask for forgiveness, and make offerings. I go to Mass because I look forward to receiving the body of Christ, and I love being surrounded by my brothers and sisters in Christ that share the same feeling.

I do not know about others, but I sometimes struggle with understanding scripture. I go to Mass because after the readings and the gospel, I love listening to the priest explain to me what scripture is really saying and how I can apply the word of God to my daily life. I go to Mass because it is the best time to ask my Father to strengthen my faith, and to help me live out the plan that He has for me. I go to Mass because I want to lead by example, and I am a blessed wife and mother. I love to go to Mass more than just on Sundays and holy days of obligation because I feel closer to God; He strengthens me, brings me joy, and prepares me for my daily struggles. I go to Mass because I want to be the daughter that God created me to be and one day, I hope to join Him in Heaven.

I GO TO MASS BECAUSE I CAN'T DO LIFE WITHOUT GOD – AND I'm not meant to. I'm grateful for His strength, mercy and love that make entering into every day possible. I was raised Catholic but didn't go to Mass much after I went away to college and came back to the Church regularly only when my daughter was born. I do have fond memories of special celebrations for feast days at my Catholic K-8 school, especially for the Blessed Mother who I simply call Mary. I'm very grateful to my parents for bringing me up Catholic. However, as a little girl, I didn't understand why there was peace for the three of us (I'm an only child) when we were in Church and unhappy chaos when we were home. My alcoholic father raged at me and my mom and she raged at him. Looking back, I know God was with me through the dysfunction. But while going through it, He mostly seemed removed.

I met the love of my life in college and we've been happily married 47 years. The joy of starting a family turned into a long, difficult recovery from postpartum depression and an anxiety disorder. It was time to face the effects of my childhood. There's nothing like major illness to turn your heart to God in the search for comfort and meaning. I was led to a 12-step group, Adult Children of Alcoholics, and slowly developed my now essential, personal relationship with God. And I learned compassion for my parents as I came to understand their own troubles. Then the Baptism of the Holy Spirit opened my heart and mind to a closer relationship with Him with more joy.

God is in charge – I'm not. Trusting Him and doing His will is the road to peace. I'm far from perfect at it but I try. He is the Source and when I go to Mass I come to the Source. I can meet Him anywhere, but to reverence His real Presence and receive Him in Communion honors Him and feeds my soul. A Catholic convert friend said recently that most Protestants might attend a church service when traveling but don't just visit churches like many Catholics do. When we go into any Catholic Church anywhere in the world – where free worship is possible – He is there. His Presence is in that place and we can feel it and know we are home. I come to Mass to come home.

I GO TO MASS BECAUSE IT BRINGS ME PEACE. I KNOW I CAN always talk to Him at any time, which I do, but being in church gives me something that is hard to explain, but it just makes me feel better.

OVER THE COURSE OF THE PAST TWO YEARS ESPECIALLY, connections are most important. It is all too easy to feel isolated even though there may be others in our homes.

I attend Mass to continue personal and spiritual connections with our Lord, to see and have the spiritual connections with the wonderful clergy at St. Mary's, and to feel a sense of community.

The daily and weekly spiritual rejuvenation makes it easier to continue to work and "socialize" via web conferences, as well as uplift our family members in the same situation in the ongoing challenges of the pandemic.

The Eucharist

"I am the Bread of Life."

— JOHN 6:48

I started to go to daily Mass because of my brother. Through his words of encouragement and example, I formed a habit of going to Mass on Fridays and Saturdays, but I was only doing it because my big brother was doing it. It wasn't until COVID that I started to appreciate the Mass.

During COVID, we were all deprived of the Mass and the Eucharist. In this loss, I started to feel this hunger in me for Jesus that would only be satisfied in the Holy Sacrifice of the Mass. My brother and I joined Bishop Barron's daily Mass livestream every morning as we excitedly awaited the day to fully participate in the liturgy. During spiritual communion, I would pray that this hunger would never be satisfied until I received Jesus in the Eucharist.

When we were finally able to go back to Mass, I wanted to

go. This longing for Mass had never been there before. During the Mass, I remember crying at different parts, but especially when I got to receive Jesus. For the first time, I understood that it was the Second Person of the Holy Trinity that I was receiving, God Himself.

Throughout summer and online school, my brother and I would still go to daily Mass. The loud longing for Mass eventually quieted, but it silently drove me to wake up early every morning, even when I didn't want to.

Recently, I started to realize that I need the Mass. I need to receive Jesus's Body, Blood, Soul, and Divinity every day because, without Him, I can do nothing. Without Him, I can't love or stay faithful. I need the graces of God and God Himself that come to me every Mass, whether I feel it or not. The words in the Mass, "Through Him, with Him, and in Him," remind me of this reality. I am meant to journey through life with Him, and it is only through Him, with Him, and in Him that I can become a saint.

Another reason I go to Mass is because the more I receive Jesus, the more I will become like Him. In Communion, the Lord dwells in me and transforms my heart to look more like His, wounds and all. This Communion is man's relationship with God. It's where God draws man to Himself, and not just to embrace Him, but to become his very food and drink. In the Eucharist, Jesus calls us to Himself to satisfy His thirst for our hearts shown on the cross. He shows us His love by making it so easy and simple to receive Him. My relationship with Christ is centered on the Mass because it's where I am closest to Him. In the Eucharist, I can embrace Jesus like Mary did in the Nativity and on the way to Calvary.

The Mass, for me, is also a call to go out and evangelize. After receiving Jesus, I pray that I may be His monstrance, that I may bring Him to those around me, like a Eucharistic procession. By going to Mass, the Lord's love and light can be brought to those who dwell in darkness. Through the graces of receiving Jesus, I have the strength to give Jesus throughout my day.

So, why do I go to Mass? I go, because I need Christ in order to love God, myself, and others. In Communion, the Lord's weary head rests on my heart, and I get to receive Him when so many have rejected Him. The Mass also provides me the grace to proclaim, through my words and actions, the good news. The Mass is a gift; a gift where Jesus vulnerably gives Himself to us in the Eucharist, asking us if we will give ourselves back.

I COME TO MASS TO RECEIVE THE BODY, BLOOD, SOUL, AND divinity of Jesus Christ. The Holy Eucharist is not just bread or wine, not just a nice image or thought, but the true fullness of Our Lord and Savior Jesus Christ. Jesus Himself tells us this in the Gospel of John:

"I am the bread of life. Your ancestors ate the manna in the desert, but they died; this is the bread that comes down from heaven so that one may eat it and not die. I am the living bread that came down from heaven; whoever eats this bread will live forever; and the bread that I will give is my flesh for the life of the world." (John 6: 48-51)

I come to Mass to receive Jesus in the Holy Eucharist so that He may live within me and I with Him. In receiving the Holy Eucharist, we become one with Him. He walks with me and I with Him. I am nothing without Him. I will never be alone after receiving Him. Jesus, Himself, instructs us:

Remain in me, as I remain in you. Just as a branch cannot bear fruit on its own unless it remains on the vine, so neither can you unless you remain in me. I am the vine, you are the branches. Whoever remains in me and I in him will bear much fruit, but without me you can do nothing. (John 15: 4-5)

I come to Mass to participate in the heavenly wedding

feast. Jesus eagerly looked forward to sharing the Passover with his disciples. In Luke's description of the Last Supper, we read that Jesus told his disciples, "I have eagerly desired to eat this Passover with you before I suffer." (Luke 22:15).

Jesus humbled Himself coming into the world to save us - you and me! Throughout the gospels He shows us His abundance of love for us and sadness at the lack of repentance by so many, but our Lord is forever merciful. Jesus talks of his desire to come into the world to set our hearts ablaze. He stated, "I have come to set the earth of fire, and how I wish it were already blazing!" (Luke 12:49). When I approach the altar to receive the Holy Eucharist, I pray that I will forever have a zeal in my heart to receive Him. Let us not be like our forefathers who grew tired of and despised the gifts of manna. We are blessed to be able to receive Him in the daily celebration of the Holy Eucharist and adore Him at Adoration.

I come to Mass to keep holy the sabbath day and participate in the Celebration of the Holy Eucharist as a member of the body of Christ. At Mount Sinai, the Lord gave Moses the Ten Commandments. The third commandment, "Remember to keep holy the sabbath day" (Exodus 20:8), is recognized in part when we come to Mass on Sundays. In Mass, we hear the word of God in the scriptures, give glory and praise to our God and take part in the heavenly banquet. We remember the Passion and Resurrection of Our Lord and Savior.

I BELIEVE THAT I WAS CREATED BY GOD AND THAT I BELONG to Him. I believe that all that I have and all that I am comes from God. I believe that ultimately, I am meant to live with Him forever (that is, to become a saint).

Scripture (His inspired Word) tells me to love Him with all my heart, soul, mind and strength (that is, with all that I have and all that I am) and to love my neighbor as myself (to strive to become like Him).

God knows and fully understands the nature of our humanity and so, to strengthen us until we can be with Him in Heaven, He gave himself to us in the Eucharist. In the ordinary scheme of things, the only place I can physically receive that precious gift is at Mass.

At each Mass I join with my brothers and sisters in Christ to step away from the world for a bit, to listen to God's Word, to give God the praise, thanks and worship that is due to Him, to receive Jesus' physical presence in the Eucharist, and then to step back into the world fortified against it.

THE MAIN REASON I GO TO MASS IS THE EUCHARIST. Receiving the actual body and blood of Christ is a profoundly wonderful experience and reveals the infinite love God continually showers upon us.

Just walking into the church provides a holy and beautiful ambiance in which to participate in the Mass, and promotes prayer and veneration to Our Lord, the Virgin Mary and the Saints.

Going to Mass truly makes me feel a part of a dynamic Catholic Community, and provides me the opportunity to "always and everywhere give thanks to the Lord."

Great homilies help me to reflect on my Faith and become closer to God, and it is incredibly inspiring to hear the most profound words for me in the Mass, other than the consecration...."may we merit to be co-heirs of eternal life!"

PERSONAL CLOSENESS WITH GOD, A CONVERSATION WITH HIM at Mass through the power of the word and the spirit is life renewing. When I visit my daughter, I attend her Bible-based Church (non-Catholic) which offers a relevant and very lively, interesting "homily" based on a chosen theme for a few weeks. This is accompanied by ramped up, spiritual band music.

My daughter thought I might be interested in joining her church but I explained to her that only in the Catholic Church do I find the deeply profound Transubstantiation of the Body and Blood of Christ, which is the soul and joy of most every Catholic.

It's the celebration of the Eucharist, the sacrifice of Jesus to save us all and the Resurrection of Our Lord which is life affirming! This is the primary motivation for me to have this magnificent communion with the community of Christ and Jesus Himself.

It unifies us as the body of Christ and glorifies God. It infuses me with a deeply fundamental belonging to know and love the God I serve which develops more faith and the hope that only the sacrifice of Jesus at the celebration of the Mass can give.

I go to Mass, first of all, for a connection with God through the Eucharist, because Jesus told us to "eat this bread" and "drink this cup," as well as "I am the vine" connecting us to real life.

I go to Mass as a believer, a worshiper - it's my identity. I have private prayer, but I also believe that Jesus wants us to live - and pray – involved in community. In community we live out our love for God, by knowing our neighbors and what we might do to help them. I go to Mass to rejoice with fellow worshipers and to be strengthened by their presence and example. I hope my presence at Mass positively impacts others too.

Strengthened by connections with these neighbors, I go

out to do whatever I can in love for the neighbors I meet in the world.

THERE ARE MANY REASONS WHY I FEEL I NEED TO PARTICIPATE in Mass on Sundays, and on every weekday that is possible for me. But the main reason dates back to a retreat I was on over 30 years ago.

I had been away from the sacraments for several years when I was in college and in my early twenties. I returned to the practice of the faith and Sunday Mass when I got engaged, and even began to volunteer in several capacities – it made me feel good to be an active participant. On this retreat, the priest gave a talk one afternoon about Our Lord hanging on the Cross, totally helpless and vulnerable, with no way to protect Himself with His hands nailed to the wood of the Cross. Yet He did this purely out of love for me. Not only did He offer his life for my salvation willingly, but He also knew I was a sinner and would continue to offend Him and increase His sufferings by my sins. This was very thought provoking; I was doing things to please the Lord and feeling good about myself for it, but had never reflected on the love that Jesus has for me, never thought of my faith as a love relationship with someone who would give everything for me *unconditionally*.

I was still pondering this new way of seeing my relationship with Jesus when our group was led into Eucharistic Adoration. This was not a completely new experience for me; growing up I experienced benediction at the end of the main Sunday Mass at the parish in the small town I was raised in. But in the small chapel on the retreat, I sat very close to the monstrance holding our Lord in the Eucharist. I began to believe in my heart what I had known in my head for many years - this *is* Jesus, the very same one who had hung upon the Cross out of love for me and for the whole world. At that moment, I truly began to love Jesus and to long for a deeper relationship with Him.

I am, of course, still a sinner and I cringe when I know I have done something to offend Him; something that weakens the relationship I long for, and I seek to be reconciled with Him frequently. Coming to Mass has become an important part of my life because it is where I can be with my Beloved and be healed and strengthened by Him every day.

WHY DO I GO TO MASS? THE EASY ANSWER IS I WAS BORN TO Catholic parents. They had me baptized as a child and I was too lazy to change. However, a number of my siblings have changed to other faiths and/or have become agnostic. So why am I still Roman Catholic?

I have found the faith to be the core of my being; it is a support and constant presence. I believe that the Lord is in the Eucharist and I do receive Him and His grace and support every time I go to communion, and every time I visit a Catholic church.

The world is constantly changing, but the Lord does not.

A SACRAMENT IS AN OUTWARD SIGN INSTITUTED BY CHRIST TO give grace, sacramental grace. For me, the sacrament of the Eucharist as THE key part of the Mass gives a special sacramental grace. Not a one-time sacrament, but one where Jesus personally lifts us up often on our daily path.

Second, I learn from the readings and the teaching of the homily, especially meanings that connect the Old and New Testament.

Third, the Mass resets my values for the days ahead.

Finally, and this is especially true on Sunday, after Mass

there is a reinforcement of faith by being present with many others even if you don't know them all personally. We are a community of faith and not alone on this journey.

IN 1994, I CAME BACK TO THE CATHOLIC CHURCH AFTER attending a "Life in the Spirit" retreat. I felt alive after rededicating my life to the Lord. Desire for the sacraments came alive in me. Receiving Jesus in the Eucharist has been a journey. The depths of His love and beauty and more are like the many facets of a diamond. The Eucharist and Scripture are the heart of my Catholic faith.

John 6:53-69: "Then Jesus said to them, 'Most assuredly I say to you, unless you eat the flesh of the son of man and drink His blood, you have no life in you. Whoever eats my flesh and drinks my blood has eternal life, and I will raise him up on the last day.'"

WHY DO I GO TO CHURCH?

Two immediate answers:

1) It is right and just, our duty and our salvation.

2) "Lord, to whom shall we go?"

On a more personal level, any decent thing I have ever done has come from spending time in church with God. Without Him, I am a base, selfish and useless creature.

My sister, who is very skeptical about religion, asked this same question last year. Here was my reply to her:

"Hi. No need to respond, but a couple weeks ago you mentioned that you believe going to church was an obsession with me and asked what I was repenting for in my past. I wanted to provide a more accurate response as my answer did the question a disservice.

I go to church because it is an amazing gift and I can think of no better, more important, or more impactful way to spend my time than worshiping the Lord, receiving the Eucharist, and praying. It has nothing to do with the past or even the future — but rather to set myself right spiritually for the day ahead."

WHEN I WAS YOUNG, MY PARENTS WERE IN A VERY ACTIVE Baptist Church. As part of their evangelism, the members would dress in costume, and go throughout our community giving little skits showing the miracles of Jesus. I was one of the little ones who was always near Jesus, and I loved being there. In this way, Jesus entered my heart as my friend and companion. He remained with me all my life, although at times He was silent. Even so, I knew He was there, waiting, to walk with me when I needed a friend, and to support me when I needed even more.

In time, as I wandered through my journey of faith, I realized I had to be even closer to Him, and through grace, I knew the way was by becoming Catholic. Now, as I go to Mass, the Jesus of my youth is with me through the Eucharist. I appreciate hearing a good homily, listening to and singing hymns, and seeing friends in the parish participate in the Mass; but the primary reason I became Catholic and go to Mass is so I may have this very special time with Jesus. Through the Eucharist, I am strengthened because Jesus is with me.

When I was young, I didn't realize what He had done for me; but I do now.

I BELIEVE THE FOUNDATIONAL TEACHING OF OUR CATHOLIC faith, that Jesus Christ, God Himself, is truly present, Body, Blood, Soul, and Divinity in the Holy Eucharist. Nothing of more eternal value will happen in the world today than the celebration of the Mass, where God Himself comes down to be with us.

When Mass is offered, undeserving though we are, He offers Himself to us, to help us in our daily struggles, to give us the grace necessary for all that He asks us to do.

I go to Mass as often as possible because I believe this reality and know that I cannot manage my life without Him.

THE REASON I COME TO MASS IS TO BE IN THE PRESENCE OF Christ in the Eucharist. In addition to keeping holy the Sabbath, I am reinvigorated for another week to go out into the world and glorify Christ by the way I live my life.

One of my college buddies used to say, in a thick Texas twang, "Church ain't a museum of saints. It's a hospital for sinners."

And, that's sums it up. I admit I'm a sinner and I need help. Each time I attend Mass I realize the other people there are admitting they are sinners, seeking salvation, and praising God for redeeming us from sin. It is a truly beautiful thing.

I go to Mass to acknowledge I am a sinner, to seek God's mercy, to receive God's graces through Holy Communion, to renew my hope in everlasting life and to join and support the other sinners slugging through life the same as me who want their hearts filled with God's love and grace.

I SPEAK WITH JESUS EVERY DAY IN MY PERSONAL PRAYERS. I also pray daily with my wife, and Jesus taught us that when two or more pray together, He is there; but the only time I am united to His true presence (Body, Blood, Soul and Divinity), is when I receive Him in the Holy Eucharist at daily or Sunday

Mass. There is no more precious a time than when I receive Him in the Blessed sacrament.

I also realize that every sin I have ever committed in my life resulted in pains for my Savior during His agony. If I fail to attend Mass every Sunday and on all Holy Days of Obligation, I would be committing yet another sin that added to His sufferings. I do not want to have added any more to His pains than I already have, so that is another reason why I go to Mass.

When I go to Mass and hear a good homily from a wise and faithful priest, it is my hope and prayer that such words will help me to grow closer to God and to do more of what He wants me to do with my life. I also hope and pray that those words will help me to better understand my faith and, so, be able to share it more efficaciously with others with whom I might interact, especially with those who are not Catholic.

And always, I remain hopeful that any graces I receive or any words I hear will help me to be a better Catholic Christian and lead me closer to God, growing in love for Him and my family, friends and others.

THOUGH THERE ARE MANY REASONS WE ATTEND MASS, HERE are the most salient points:

- We can start the day with Christ in mind; thanking Him for providing us another opportunity to glorify Him and serve those whom we will encounter throughout the day.
- We can bask in His presence, in the silence the church offers, and enter in a personal conversation with Him in prayer asking for guidance on the

myriad opportunities and/or issues we will
confront on a daily basis.

- We can ask Him for forgiveness for our
transgressions and/or wrongs we have committed.
We can ask Him to give us the strength to
overcome the temptations of the devil and to
provide us the resilience to live our lives according
to His will.

- We can enjoy the opportunity the Catholic Church
provides us to witness and participate, on a daily
basis, Heaven on earth, as articulated by Saint
John Paul II and described in Scott Hahn's book,
"The Lamb's Supper," through the celebration of
the holy Mass. After all, the Eucharist is the source
and summit of our Catholic faith.

I GO TO SUNDAY MASS AND DAILY MASS AS OFTEN AS I AM
able. The reason I go to Mass is the deep desire within me to
start my day in Jesus' presence; most importantly to receive
Jesus in the Most Holy Eucharist and receive the graces He
offers me at that very moment.

When I receive the Most Holy Eucharist, I thank Him and
the Holy Spirit for His graces and pray that His thoughts, be my
thoughts that day, His words, be the words that cross my lips that
day, and His deeds, be the deeds I do that day. I offer up everything I think, say and do for Him at every moment, second…of
the day and that I see Him in everyone I meet that day.

I come to Him at Mass to thank Him for all the many
miracles He gives me each and every day and night. (I always
thank Him at the very moment of each miracle He gives me
each day.) I bring to Jesus my sorrows for those whom I ask
Him for His mercy in granting my prayers of need for all

those that I keep in my heart, the living, the dead, those who are physically sick and those who are spiritually in need, the end to abortion, and all those that have asked for my prayers.

I have found that alone I cannot handle all the many troubles in my life, so at Mass I surrender to Jesus, everything going on in my life, in my heart, in my mind, my body, my soul, and all life's problems and sorrows. I give everything to Jesus' compassionate care and surrender all my hurt, pain, worry, doubt, fear and anxiety, and when I leave Mass, I leave with the most wonderful, the most serene feeling knowing that Our Lord is totally in charge of my life that day.

It is such a wonderful feeling to see the many faces of so many faithful Catholics at Mass as they too come to worship our Lord. Knowing we all come to share in the Most Holy Eucharist together.

He is always waiting for me at every Mass.

ONE SHOULD GO TO MASS FOR THE BENEFIT OF THEIR OWN soul. When you go to Mass you receive Jesus Christ our Lord and Savior into your body, which gives you an astounding amount of grace from God. You also got a chance to participate in the Mass which essentially is Christ's sacrifice for us.

Many miracles and changing of people's lives have occurred at Mass, which shows the immense importance of going to Mass and receiving the Eucharist.

THIRTY-FIVE YEARS AGO, I TOOK A THEOLOGY COURSE AT Boston College, and we were discussing a sermon written by the German Lutheran theologian, the Reverend Dr. Paul Tillich. The subject was sin, and Dr. Tillich expounded on how sin created a "separateness" between man and God.

When we sin, we isolate ourselves from God's love and mercy, and sin prevents us from developing a relationship with Him. That lesson and the idea of being separated from God because of sin has always stayed with me.

While Dr. Tillich was talking about sin, the same is true about weekly Mass. On those rare occasions when I have chosen not to attend Mass and not receive Holy Communion, that "separateness" becomes real. The sense of missing something important is felt, and the realization that I created a space between myself and Jesus is palpable. By not attending, I find there is a small spiritual hole that can't be filled in the material world.

There certainly are irritants that can happen at Mass: Hymns no one has ever sung, cantors who think they are the entertainment portion of the Mass, or the 25-minute meandering sermon. We all have our pet peeves, and I have used them as excuses to not attend Mass. But when I've used them, and compare them to what I am missing, those excuses are small and petty. The purpose of the Mass is not the music, the cantor, or even the priest's sermon (except our Pastor's!) The centrality of the Mass is hearing the Word of God and receiving the Eucharist. I need those things, not just for my immortal soul, but to fill that spiritual need of being close to, and not separated from, God.

I WOULD RECOMMEND GOING TO MASS BECAUSE IT'S THE easiest way to get grace. As I have grown older, I have noticed that you cannot rely on just yourself to overcome sin, because we are fallen, and the devil is so much smarter than we are. But when you receive the Eucharist often, it is not just you versus the devil, it's you and Christ within you versus the devil, and we know from scripture that Christ is smarter and more powerful than the devil.

Mass is also a great way to physically participate in the faith. While silent prayer is good, it is often hard to do because we are material entities. So, in the Mass we not only participate spiritually but also physically in the reception of the Eucharist.

I ATTEND MASS TO ENCOUNTER AND RECEIVE THE LIVING GOD. He tells us in scripture how He wants to be worshiped. We're told to celebrate the Eucharist together in remembrance of Him. "Where two or more are gathered in my name, there am I in their midst." Solitary prayer is certainly good; Jesus did it, but He also tells us to pray in community. We're strengthened when we pray together and we aren't meant to be spiritual lone rangers.

The Mass is the perfect prayer as it begins with repentance for sin, then prayers of petition, thanksgiving, and praise followed by hearing and feeding on His Word in scripture. The culmination is receiving Him spiritually and physically in Holy Communion. It's the perfect prayer and a foretaste of our union with Him in Heaven.

WHY DO I GO TO MASS? WHAT A QUESTION! AS I STARTED writing about the reasons I go to Mass, I found myself with an extensive list. I probably could have googled and found a similar one. Eventually I realized other people's observations of me might say it better than my myriad of reasons.

I work in the Pentagon where we have daily Mass at lunchtime. I try to get to that Mass at least a few times a week (or did pre-pandemic). I never know if I'll be sitting next to a general or a janitor, but we are all equal and welcome. And we all actively recognize each other throughout the building and wave or smile knowingly to each other in the hallways or in a meeting. One day after I discovered someone had yet again scheduled a meeting during Mass time, a non-religious co-worker suggested I put Mass on my calendar every day to discourage others in the office from scheduling me during that time. My hesitation to do it was met with, "Please?! I prefer to work with you when you've been to Mass." Wow! There really was so much of a difference in me that people noticed. Wow.

Story two: One warm February day I opted to walk back to my office from lunchtime Mass through the courtyard. When I arrived in our office space, I announced it was a beautiful day and everyone should take a few minutes to get some sunshine and fresh air. Two of the folks that were right there were pouring over a document on the computer. One of them had started going to daily Mass occasionally when he joined our organization. Some days he'd even catch me early in the morning and ask if I were going to Mass that day to find him and bring him along as he anticipated a tough day. Well, he looked up at me that day as I came in, and he exclaimed, "You are absolutely glowing! You must have just been to Mass."

Whether I go to Mass out of obligation or as a social outlet or for the Eucharist or because it's part of who I am or for any of a number of REASONS I do, Mass and everything with it makes me a better person, a better child of God who can deal with life more calmly, more lovingly, more focused than I would otherwise. I believe that version of me is a glimpse of what God sees and plans for me to be.

I RECOMMEND — AND, IN TURN — ATTEND THE MASS FOR THREE reasons: temporal, spiritual, and dutiful.

The temporal reason is fulfillment. I love to start my days by waking early up early and participating in the Mass. It makes me happy and there is a feeling of contentment to begin my day on a good note.

The spiritual reason is grace. The reception of the Holy Eucharist so vital for our perfection, and also administers an abundance of graces.

The dutiful reason is my purpose as a human being. I was created by the almighty God to know love and serve Him in this life and be happy with and praise Him forever in the next. There is no better way to adore God than going to His house and praying the way He handed to us: the Mass!

WHY DO I GO TO MASS? NOT AS SIMPLE A QUESTION AS I first thought. My reasons have changed over the years. At the present time I attend Sunday Mass because I have accepted the belief that it is a sin not to. The Third Commandment says to Keep Holy the Sabbath Day. Since I have chosen Catholicism as my religion, it is only logical that I try to follow the teachings of the Catholic Church. Catholicism teaches that it's a sin to miss Mass on Sunday without good reason. Even if I can't attend in person, I can certainly watch the Mass on the internet; and, if I can't I do that, I can set aside some time every Sunday to reflect on the blessings of God and thank Him for all that I have.

But there are other reasons too. So, here's the chronological list of how I came to my current rationale for attending Mass EVERY Sunday.

1. **Because that's what I was told to do.** I was told to go to church every Sunday (but it wasn't Catholic Mass). I was raised in the Episcopal Church because my grandfather and father were Episcopal priests. I went to church on Sunday

simply because my father told me to. Missing Sunday services was not an option.

2. **Because I didn't want spend any more time than was absolutely necessary with my Drill Instructor, D.I.).** After leaving home for college and then joining the Navy, my attendance at Sunday church services became more sporadic. The rationalizations for skipping came more easily. But on my first Sunday at officer's candidate school (boot camp), my Marine Corps Drill Instructor gave me a choice. I could attend the Catholic Mass, or Protestant Sunday Service, or Jewish Service, OR I could spend the time with my D.I. engaging in extra military instruction. I needed a break from my D.I. so it was either the Priest, the Minister or a Rabbi for me. Now as an Episcopalian I knew that Jewish services were probably not where I should be. I knew I wasn't Catholic, but I had no idea what a Protestant was. So, I asked the base chaplain where the Episcopalians should be. Right or wrong, the chaplain told me that if I truly believed the Eucharist was the Body and Blood of Christ, I should probably attend Catholic Mass. So, I did. And every Sunday I had the same desire to distance myself from my Drill Instructor, so I found myself at Mass.

3. **For my wife.** Boot camp didn't last forever and neither did my need to go to Mass. However, shortly after boot camp I met someone I wanted to spend time with and she was a devout Catholic. So back to Mass I went.

4. **It was part of the "Agreement."** When my wife agreed to marry me, we also agreed that we would do so in a Catholic church. During my pre-

cana classes I made a commitment to give Catholicism my "best effort," and that meant attending Mass every Sunday.

5. **To win the test of my devotion to my Catholic commitment.** I'm a fairly competitive person. I like a good challenge. Was it possible to attend Mass every Sunday? Well, it's easy to meet that challenge if you have complete control over your life and more importantly, your schedule. Unfortunately, as a young naval officer, I did not have such control. The needs of the Navy always came first. My time was quite simply, not my own. However, at every naval base and ship I served on, throughout my career, there was a church and a Catholic priest. And my Sunday commitment could be met anywhere from 1600 on Saturday through 1800 on Sunday. It was very rare that the needs of the Navy were so constricting that I couldn't find at least one Mass to attend during that timeframe. I learned early in my Catholic life that the Catholics were very serious about Sunday Mass, and the Universal Catholic Church provided far more opportunity to meet one's Sunday obligations that the Episcopal Church ever did.

6. **Because I wanted to.** I don't remember when it actually happened, but somewhere in all those weeks of Sunday Mass, I realized that attending wasn't such a chore, or challenge or hardship. I actually wanted to attend. Maybe it was because I wanted something from God. It wasn't enough that I attend just because it was sinful not to. Attending Mass become a great opportunity to not only thank God for what I had, but to ask for help with my needs and desires at the time. It always struck me as odd, when I heard people say they didn't

attend Mass anymore because they didn't get anything out of the Mass. I never thought much about what I got out of the Mass. I thought the obligation to attend was more about what you were supposed to put INTO the Mass rather than what you got back.

7. **As an example for my children.** It turned out the Navy was pretty good about teaching the concept of leadership by example. With the blessings of children, it was only logical that if I wanted them to become good Catholics, I needed to show them the way. Kids can be pretty relentless in their efforts to avoid things they don't really want to do. It takes some kids longer than others to understand the importance of attending Sunday Mass "religiously." My kids complained that they simply didn't LIKE going to Mass (for a variety of reasons). My response was simply, "No child LIKES going to Mass. But unless you need to go the emergency room, you're going anyway!" The inevitability of the situation seemed to end that particular argument. The kids would go because I told them to. The rest of the reasons why, they would learn on their own…with the help of the Catholic Church, the priests, and Sunday school.

So, there you have it. Why do I go to Sunday Mass? Because it's the right thing to do and it's probably the easiest obligation God asks of us.

Post Script:

I know I'm long-winded and have certainly offered more than you asked. However, there are a couple of other events in my life that helped cement that rationale I outlined above for attending Mass every Sunday.

I can't emphasize enough my appreciation for how serious

the Catholic Church insists on every Catholic attending Mass every Sunday. I think I have been given an opportunity that most Catholics have not. Because of my Navy career and my follow-on career as an airline pilot, I have found myself away from home on Sundays MORE times than not. For most of my adult life, I believe it has been a tad bit harder for me than most Catholics to meet my Sunday obligation. But the point I want to make is that it wasn't as hard as I thought. When your career choices force you to travel (a lot), you really get an appreciation for the breadth of the Universal Catholic Church. Of course, in my many Sundays spent away from home within the United States, it wasn't too difficult to find a convenient Catholic Church. Even when I was in the predominately Baptist area of the deep southern states or the highly Mormon area of Utah, Catholic Churches were simply not that hard to locate. But the really impressive times were when I found myself in Bucharest, Egypt, Moscow or Ghana. All I did was is talk to the concierge. Sure enough, in all those places the closest Catholic Church was not very far away. Many times, commuting to Mass was easier and more convenient than when I'm in my home town! Of course, during overseas travel it's rare to find the Mass in English. But with the help of my daily Missal, about the only thing I couldn't comprehend at a foreign Mass was the homily. And then there were the times I went on an 11-day high adventure backpacking trip with the Boy Scouts. How to do you attend Mass in the backcountry of the Rocky Mountains? The answer is, you can't. However, the Catholic Church found a very reasonable alternative solution to this challenge. The local bishop said that if you attend a daily Mass service on the day before you leave on your trek, AND attend a daily Mass service on the day you return from your trek, then you will have met your Sunday obligation. Now I don't know if the local bishop had the authority to do what he did. It doesn't matter. Again, the point is, the Catholic Church is very serious about Sunday obligation. And if you're honest with yourself, you really have to work hard to find a true excuse for NOT attending. Wherever you are in the world, there is a Mass available. Attending is easy.

Ok, so attending Mass is easy. But, why do it? Certainly not just because it's easy or because someone else tells you that you should; right? I guess it all boils down to faith. I believe that all Christian religions are "faith based." There's no absolute guarantee that what Christianity teaches is completely true…and certainly not provable beyond any doubt. If it were, then "faith" would not be required. Two plus three equals five, and the sun rises in the East. You don't need faith to believe facts. Those two facts are true regardless of whether you have faith in them or not.

So where does one get faith? Well, for me there were events that helped establish my faith that God exists. I'll only bore you further with one. It was a sermon I heard, telling the story about the watch on the moon. (I don't know if anyone else has heard this story. Perhaps it's much more common than I'm thinking.) Anyway, the story presents a question. Suppose you are Neil Armstrong and you are just taking the first steps of any human being on the face of the moon. After your third step you look down and you see a wrist watch. What would be your thoughts? Would you think the watch just magically materialized from the elements on the moon? That certainly doesn't seem logical. Even though the elements to produce the watch are present on the moon, to think those elements randomly arranged themselves over eons of time into the familiar object of a wrist watch, would, in my opinion, be nonsense. Although some I suppose might have the faith that such a thing could happen. A more rational excuse for the presence of the watch is that Neil Armstrong, is NOT the first human on the moon. Someone had obviously been there before him. If Neil didn't drop the watch, then someone else did. It didn't just happen to appear.

Now the universe as we know it, is certainly far more complex than a simple wrist watch. And if the wrist watch didn't just magically appear out of nowhere, than neither did the universe. Just like man produced the wrist watch, some other person or being produced the universe. And that person/being we refer to as God. It takes a little faith to believe God exists. And it takes a little more faith to believe the Catholic Church teaches the truth about who God is and what God expects of us. So, if you want to decide if the Catholic Church has it right…go to Sunday Mass and find out for yourself. It's the right thing to do, and it is easy.

WHY DO I ATTEND MASS? GOOD QUESTION! I HAVE NOT really thought about why I go; I just go. For most of my adult life I usually made it to Mass on Sunday. However, I started attending daily Mass in 1995, after arriving in the Philippines for a two year unaccompanied tour and needed something to occupy my alone time. I started with sports: tennis, racquetball, softball, swimming and golf; they were good but did not satisfy my loneliness.

A Catholic hospital that was within walking distance from where I was living had Sunday Mass, so I would attend Mass there on Sundays. They also had a 6:00 a.m. daily Mass. Since I worked nearby, I thought I could attend Mass and still make my 7:30 start time. So, I tried it. Well, I guess I was missing starting my day with God. Within a few days I wasn't as lonely and my days seemed to be moving right along. In fact, that two years just slipped away. Guess I was missing a relationship with God all along, and being alone brought it to the front.

I still attend daily Mass. It has become a part of my daily routine. Now when I miss Mass, I feel like something is lacking in my day. There are little things that don't feel quite right. All I know is that my day feels less fulfilling. I need my daily fix of

God: to worship, adore and welcome His saving grace. But mostly I need the graces from receiving the Eucharist and Precious Blood each day.

I GO TO MASS BECAUSE I LOVE GOD.

How does anyone treat someone they love? One way is to spend time with that person. So, I do.

Another way is to have a conversation with that person, talking to him and listening to him.

Having someone you love means you have an intimate, unique relationship with them like you would with a parent, sibling, spouse, or close friend. I experience that relationship during Mass.

But there's more. He, our Lord, during Mass wants me to eat His body and drink His blood. Why? Because He said, "I myself am the living bread come down from Heaven. If anyone eats this bread he shall live forever; the bread I will give is my flesh, for the life of the world." (John 6:51). What could be more intimate than this?

I GO TO MASS TO HAVE A PERSONAL CLOSENESS WITH GOD, A conversation with Him at Mass through the power of the Word and the Spirit. It is life renewing. Only in the Catholic Church do I find the deeply profound transubstantiation of the Body and Blood of Christ which is the soul and joy of most every Catholic.

It's the celebration of the Eucharist, the sacrifice of Jesus to save us all, and the Resurrection of Our Lord which is life affirming! This is the primary motivation for me to have this magnificent communion with the community of Christ and Jesus Himself.

It unifies us as the body of Christ and glorifies God. It infuses me with a deeply fundamental belonging to know and love the God I serve which develops more faith and the hope that only the sacrifice of Jesus at the celebration of the Mass can give.

I LOVE TO GO TO MASS AND RECOMMEND GOING TO MASS because God is truly present there. At every Mass Jesus is physically present in the Eucharist, no matter what is going on in your life, how dry your prayer feels or how alone you are. God is there and He loves you.

So many times, when I have gone to Mass with whatever feeling or problem I have, I have been able to give it to Him and receive Him in return.

I GO TO MASS BECAUSE JESUS IS THERE IN THE EUCHARIST. God is infinite and all-powerful, but out of pure generosity, He comes to us in the humblest of forms - a seemingly bland piece of bread - and then He lets us receive Himself *into our bodies*. We get to gaze upon His face in adoration, which is incredible enough, but then He actually calls us to consume Him in a gift of His entire self. It inspires me to give my entire self back to Jesus.

When I go to Mass, I sometimes have trouble paying attention. But I persevere because I know God's love for me is not contingent on how well I mentally process every second, or how emotionally shaken I am by one particular moment. I know that all I need to do is come before Him in a state of grace, ready to humbly admit my own weakness and my need for Him. Sure enough, He comes to me every time - in His word, in His mercy, and best of all in the Blessed Sacrament.

I've grown to appreciate the gift of attending Mass more than just on Sundays because of how it changes my day and my week when I am frequently enriched with God's gift of himself. I've found that when I view Mass as a gift and not as a chore, it takes on a whole new meaning and fills my life with joy.

I DON'T GO TO MASS BECAUSE I AM SUPPOSED TO. I DON'T GO to Mass out of habit. I don't go to Mass because it makes me feel good. I don't go to Mass because I want to. I go to Mass for one reason…I go to Mass to be with Jesus.

More acutely, I go to Mass to receive the Eucharist. The crux of our faith, the most incredible grace imaginable is to be able to receive the Eucharist and truly be united with Christ. This wonder is only available at Mass. It is why I attend and why it was so heartbreaking to not be able to attend earlier in the pandemic. I am whole with Christ.

I am so grateful to be Catholic and to be able to experience this; I pray that all can share in this joy.

I GO TO MASS TO CONSUME THE LIVING GOD WHO'S SO unthinkably immense Heaven itself cannot contain! But God makes Himself small enough for me, a poor sinner, to be privileged to be able to receive Him, Body, Blood, Soul, and Divinity…all that into the depths of my heart and soul at every Mass!

It's so amazing how we can receive Jesus at the Holy Sacrifice of the Mass and to converse closely with Jesus, seconds after Holy Communion! And the only people who can make this possible are our beloved priests! No priest, no Mass, no Jesus!

JESUS, in the Most Blessed Sacrament, is our and the Catholic Church's greatest and unequaled treasure! You are missing out on something truly wonderous if you choose not to go to Mass. Jesus and our Blessed Mother are there, always present! It is an experience of Heaven on Earth! It's our opportunity to worship and thank God for all the graces and blessings we have been given!

Going to Mass is not an obligation, or a duty. For me it is vital and essential to my spiritual well-being and it keeps my intimate personal relationship with Jesus thriving!

✠

Why I go to Mass: because God loves me.

I want to love God.

Where else can I can I get so close to God that I am able to actually have Him physically present in my body? The Lord's Body, Blood, Soul and Divinity in me and as a part for me, at least for a while. Jesus Christ is in me when I partake of the Eucharist. Besides this being almost beyond belief it is true because He said so.

When you love someone, you want to please them. God loves me, and when I am at Mass I am pleased to be there. Here He pleases me in many of the traditional ways: thanking Him for all I received; hearing His words and His Word; getting an explanation or encouragement from the homily; presenting my petitions for those I love - my family, my friends and often, the world, and for our faith and salvation; being in the church as the priest says those words of Christ and what looks to be bread and wine do become Him who saves us; receiving Him in the Eucharist; and receiving the blessing and grace needed to go forth into the world; and leaving Mass to be His witness. He gives me all I need for that, but I often fall short or fail. So back to Mass I go.

At Mass we are gathered as a community. Christ asks us to

be together as His Church. Where better than to be with Him during the Sacrifice of the Mass? We pray for each other; that is powerful because where we are, Christ is with us, lovingly hearing us.

As Catholics we have been given this great liturgy. God gave it to us so we can experience and realize how much He loves us in sacrificing Himself for us. How He sacrificed Himself for our salvation. So we can be with Him forever. Sharing the love of the Trinity. That is how I believe He wishes us to worship Him. It is the greatest way He shows how much He loves us by giving His life for us.

Not every morning do I get up and go to Mass with this state of mind and focus on the Lord. But He gets me up, draws me there knowing I'm a work in progress. Lots of progress is needed. But He loves each of us. I want to love Him and partaking in the Mass helps. Each time I am there I am as close as I can get to Him to tell Him that I love Him. So, back to Mass I go.

MASS IS THE ONLY WAY I WANT TO START MY DAY, TO GET ME focused on what is really important.

Eucharist – To experience the immensity of God's love, that He would send His Son to die for me. To humble Himself to become present in a piece of bread so that I can know that He is present within me, leading me, directing me, supporting me, helping me in all that I do.

I AM NEVER ALONE. He helps me to see the beauty in the world, in the people around me.

He teaches me to be joyful, to rejoice in all things, knowing that He turns all things to good.

It is a wonderful opportunity to share Christ's presence with others.

I truly appreciate Mass being streamed on-line for the days that I am not physically able to attend.

THE SHORT ANSWER IS THAT I ATTEND MASS BECAUSE THAT IS where I need to be. Spiritually, emotionally, and mentally; Mass provides me a reminder of what is important and keeps me grounded.

I have fallen in love with the Eucharistic Prayer. The transubstantiation of the host and the wine is, in my view, one of the most beautiful sights I have ever experienced. Even when I could only attend Mass on-line during COVID, as appreciated as that was, I felt left out of the experience and unable to experience the true beauty of it.

THERE HAVE BEEN SOME TIMES IN MY WALK THROUGH LIFE where I have gone to Mass only because of the obligation to attend weekly Mass. And for those times I am thankful for the obligation. As I think about it now though, a number of blessings of Mass jump out at me. One blessing that became much more apparent during the pandemic is how blessed we are to be able to receive the Eucharist and attend Mass in person on a regular basis.

Other blessings that draw me to Mass are to hear the Word of God proclaimed, to be spiritually strengthened on a regular basis, to have communion with others in the Body of Christ, and to have the blessing in my walk of a persistent reiterative close time with Our Lord.

WHY DO I GO TO MASS? BECAUSE IT IS AN ESSENTIAL PART OF my life. The Sacred Heart of Jesus and the Immaculate Heart of the Blessed Virgin Mary are engraved in my heart!

Attending Mass is a precious way and opportunity to thank God for everything and for the Divine Love we receive in Holy Communion. Amen.

MY REASONS TO GO TO MASS EVERY SUNDAY, AND EVEN DAILY, are three-fold:

First, Faith. I believe in the teaching of our Catholic Church that the Eucharist is the source and summit of our faith, the center of our faith. I believe that Jesus' Body, Blood, Soul and Divinity is present in every host I receive at Holy Communion. Therefore, Jesus, my love and my hope, is the ultimate nourishment for my soul and the surest way to reach my goal of union with God.

Christ desires for us to attend Mass, to be really present to Him, to love Him, to adore Him, to receive Him and thereby become more and more like Him. Mass is also the supreme way of giving praise to the Father, in thanksgiving for all creation and for salvation.

In growing up as a cradle Catholic, I did not understand the lofty sacrifice of the Mass. It was all too easy to look at Mass as a Sunday obligation that could be skipped for social reasons or sport events.

Second, Family. I enjoy being at Mass in communion with so many others, all children of God who also pray and receive and give thanks to our loving, generous and merciful God. We are God's family. Jesus took on human nature to save us but also to communicate with us, and to show us how to live in the Kingdom of God.

Third, Service. St. Mary of Sorrows parish is outstanding in its service to God, to neighbor, and to the poor. Attending

Mass, listening to announcements and reading the bulletin, I learn about the needs of others. I have the opportunity to choose from a multitude of ministries to get involved in, to help my neighbor and to live the Christian life.

It took me many years to appreciate more and more my Catholic faith, the Church, the community of the faithful and most of all, Holy Mass. As one who surely has lived most of her earthly life, I am filled with joy and gratitude for the grace of the Eucharist, the Bread of life, the sacrament of Holy Mass.

Jesus

I am a daily Mass attendee and member of St. Clare's who retired out of the area. However, I was forced out of retirement and am back in Fairfax indefinitely and attend the 6:30 a.m. morning Mass at St. Mary of Sorrows. I didn't get your email but heard your request this morning to give you feedback on why I attend daily Mass.

By the grace of God, I became a Supernumerary in Opus Dei 45 years ago and have been attending daily Mass since then as part of my plan of life. While that got me started, that is far down on the list why I attend daily Mass now. It does give me the opportunity to practice obedience which I need to help me pursue the ever-elusive virtue of humility.

The main reason I attend daily Mass is that I'm in love with Jesus in the Blessed sacrament, and the Sacrifice of the Mass - the highest form of prayer - is the best way I know of to pursue and experience union with the One I love. For me, a father of seven children who deeply loves my wife, to receive Him in Communion is spiritual consummation of a relationship tantamount to consummation of the marriage vows. My daily prayer is for grace to love Him more, thank Him for everything, beg for mercy and the virtue of humility, and to be used by Him.

I would have to write a book to explain more fully the other reasons for attending daily Mass from praise, thanksgiving, grace to struggle to grow in virtue, presence of God, etc. It's like asking a man madly in love with his wife why do you spend time with her every day? The lover wants to be with the beloved and a day without the Mass has a giant hole in it.

May Our Lord and Our Lady continue to shower you with blessings in every way; my apologies for the long windedness, but I am also madly in love with the Church and her faithful priests.

I GO TO MASS TO RENEW AND STRENGTHEN MY ONGOING communion with Jesus and the universe He has and continues to create.

As I live and renew this communion during Mass:

I say a "Yes" to all which, over time, I gradually perceive God is asking of me. Often, I begin to sense what it is from a scripture reading or a sermon message.

I say "Thank you" for the whole of Jesus' creation whether it be in the far reaches of the cosmos, the very pew in which I sit or the others sitting with me. I say "Thank you" for the blessings and labors, known and unknown, which God lovingly showers upon us all.

I say "Please," asking that God give me, our parish, and all creatures here and elsewhere, an ever-increasing sense of gratitude for this creation. I ask for a gradual increase in our miniscule understanding of its ultimate purpose.

Lastly, as I prepare with others to reaffirm my communion with Jesus and, through Him, with them, we pray, "Thy will be done on earth as it is in Heaven."

I will never understand all that God is up to. Nevertheless, with childlike trust, I pray with those around me and, indeed, with all humankind, that God's will be done not just at St. Mary's but throughout the earth…as it is in Heaven.

That's why I go to Mass. So that my fellow believers and I can joyfully say to Jesus, each in his or her own way: "Yes," "Thank you," "Please," and "Thy will be done."

I GO TO MASS AND RECOMMEND THE MASS TO OTHERS because it is the best way that a Catholic can grow close to God. We cannot gain eternal life except through Christ. We must grow in our faith and become more like Christ each day and the best way we can do that is by receiving His Body, Blood, Soul and Divinity at the holy sacrifice of the Mass.

Another reason I would recommend the Mass to others is because we, as Catholics living 2,000 years after the life of Christ, did not get to personally witness the ultimate sacrifice Christ made to redeem us. The Holy Mass is our way in participating at Calvary.

I HAVE HAD AN OPPORTUNITY TO READ MANY OF THE submissions answering "Why do you go to Mass?" and it is marvelous to read the beautiful testimonies regarding finding Jesus there, gaining His strength, and having an opportunity to worship and adore Him. They are beautiful statements of faith.

I don't know about you but sometimes no matter how much I would like to pretend otherwise, I struggle with my faith. What is it I believe? Why is this not easier? I get confused, feel lost and want to just give up. "I'm just not good enough; maybe I don't belong here."

Those are the times I most need to go to Mass. Those times of confusion are when I most need to go to Him. He can handle my confusion. He can handle my doubts. I actually don't need to have all the answers when I walk thorough those doors! Just walking in can be a tremendous "yes" to His invitation. And with each "yes," I get closer to genuine answers, not temporary ones. Just walking through those doors means I am more open to the healing He provides, the strength He wants too share, the love He gives me always.

Even when I don't feel it.

Life is hard and complicated and often there are difficult questions where it's hard to see a way out of uncomfortable, even painful situations. Going to Mass does not "fix" these situations; it doesn't necessarily answer our questions. But going to Mass can make it easier to breathe, to help me realize I'm not alone even when I feel alone; it gives me an opportunity to rest in Him, and take Him with me when I leave.

When I am lost, going to Mass can help me remember that He knows where I am. I am not lost to Him. He is right there. He knows that I don't have the answers. I only have questions.

Why do I go to Mass? Sometimes I go because life is hard and if I listen with my often-confused heart, I can hear His "I know" and His "I'm with you."

AS ONE WHO AT ONE TIME INFREQUENTLY ATTENDED CHURCH, I understand the attraction of being reluctant to going to church and just being "a good person." I now attend Mass regularly and have found a constant strength and direction in life.

Previously my thoughts had been: I can pray anywhere anytime. I can use that hour or so to do other things. I'm a pretty good person anyway. The Mass just doesn't have much meaning for me.

Jesus spoke in parables, so I am offering an analogy comparing maintaining our cars to maintaining our souls. On one hand this is a ridiculous comparison, but similar problems can occur with each.

Most people rely on their automobile to get them places safely each day. These cars need attention to maintain their safety and utility as in the following four examples:

- When the car seems to wander over the road pulling to one side or another, the car needs alignment.
- When the car seems to skid, the tires need to be replaced.
- When it is difficult to see the road, the headlights need to be replaced.
- When a warning light comes on, the oil and filter may need to be replaced or the tires may need to be inflated.

These repairs don't work when attempted at home. The symptoms need a reliable trained mechanic to diagnose and get the car back on the road working properly.

1. Just like a car, the soul needs realignment to keep us from wandering.
2. When our days seem to be out of control, our priorities need to be assessed.
3. When we can't see which way to go, our goals need to be established.

4. When life seems to be sending us warnings, we
   need to stop and figure out why.

Finding a reliable repair shop is essential for our cars' welfare. Going to church is essential for our souls' welfare. Jesus is a "master mechanic" unequaled in repairing our lives. In Mass, the priest acts in the person of Christ – listen to him. The bible has numerous examples of God's warnings. It is incredible how these biblical readings at Mass seem to relate to warning signs in our lives. At Mass the Liturgy of the Word and homily help diagnose our weaknesses. Reflection in front of the tabernacle or at Adoration will give us direction; the priest provides forgiveness and direction in confession; Jesus will provide direction; if we only listen to Him, we will understand that "we are not alone."

What's going on in the different parts of the Mass may not be obvious. There are CDs and literature that will help us understand God's sacrifices and love and realize our offerings and blessings. Nowhere else can we be part of the priest acting in the person of Christ changing ordinary bread and wine into the actual body and blood of Christ.

Jesus is waiting for you, and will welcome you with open arms.

I HAVE GONE TO DAILY MASS FOR OVER 30 YEARS BECAUSE I absolutely believe what Jesus told us in the "Bread of Life" discourse in Chapter 6 of John's Gospel. I believe it to be the most important teaching Jesus taught...or His biggest lie, which I do _not_ believe it to be.

Jesus said it. I believe it. That settles it.

I want to go to Heaven when I die and this is the best way to get there, in my opinion.

As an aside, my wife became a Catholic five years after going to Mass with me. She is in Heaven now.

THE BIGGEST INFLUENCE ON MY GOING TO MASS WAS MY father. He made sure that my sisters and I attended Catholic schools and were brought up in the faith. He also walked the walk by attending Mass every Sunday and Holy Day of Obligation. It was something that was important to him and therefore became important to me.

"Why do I go to Mass?" I have been asked this question several times in my life, mainly when I was in my 20's and early 30's. I always started my answer by asking the person asking the question one of a series of questions. Why do you exercise? Why do you watch what you eat? Why did you go to school? I would often get the usual answers: I want to stay healthy and I have a desire to know and understand how and why things work. I would then tell them I go to Mass for the same reasons. Attending Mass is exercise and nourishment for the mind and soul. The Word of God proclaimed helps me to better understand the broken world in which we live and causes me to inspect my thoughts and actions, and make course corrections where necessary. Communion feeds my soul with the new bread from Heaven, the Body and Blood of Jesus Christ, the son of God. So, I go for exercise and food for my soul.

Often, the questioners walked away. I suppose they thought I was a little weird for being Catholic and attending Mass every Sunday, but I never cared what they thought. Instead, I would say a prayer for them so they could someday feel how I feel when I am at Mass.

I GO TO MASS TO BE UNITED WITH THE MYSTICAL BODY OF Christ which includes all Christians with Christ as the Head.

At Mass, I am encouraged to unite with other Christians in prayer and praise. I am also encouraged to participate in the mission of the Church, to spread the gospel and to perform good works in the name of Jesus Christ.

I RECOMMEND ATTENDING MASS BECAUSE IT IS WHERE WE CAN participate in one of the greatest sacraments. You get to receive Jesus in the form of bread. It is crazy to think that you can actually do that, but God made it possible. When I go to Mass, Jesus overflows His graces on me. I get to receive Him and be filled with His love and blessings.

Going to Mass is an amazing way to grow in your faith and relationship with Our Lord Jesus Christ. At Mass you hear in the readings about all the amazing things Jesus did in his life and we can learn from His example of how we can lead a better life.

I GO TO MASS BECAUSE I PROFESS TO BE A FOLLOWER OF JESUS. He said "Do this in remembrance of me" at the Last Supper and the Mass is a reenactment of the Last Supper in response to His request.

There are, of course, other reasons: to hear the homily, to gather with others who follow Jesus, to pray with music, or because the church is a good place for prayer. But these reasons cannot be the major inducement to attend, because at some point, they will all fail. Homilies vary and even a good one may fail because of your mood that day or poor sound quality. The other people in attendance, including the clergy, are Christians and so by definition imperfect and in need of salvation. The music varies and even if you agree with the music director's interpretation, the parish may someday change the music director. On any given day, the building may or may not be conducive to prayer depending on the individual and the number of distractions, and in any case the building is temporary. In general, the things that make me feel good will often be absent.

If I want to have good feelings, I can watch the Hallmark Channel. If I want to move toward being a better Christian, I should listen to Jesus.

Jesus told us, "Do this in memory of me."

By attending the Holy Sacrifice of the Mass, we encounter God and His people most intimately.

In joining with other Catholics (the Body of Christ) we acknowledge that God is present with us as together we hear His word and pray in petition, praise and thanksgiving. By receiving the real presence of Our Divine Lord through Holy Communion, we are truly united with Him. We memorialize His sacrifice on the Cross and receive the graces from this sacrament which we pray will enable us to better reflect His presence in our daily lives at all times.

Mass is our means to grow closer to God; we are so very blessed for this heavenly opportunity and should gratefully accept this gift.

I go to Mass because I believe in Jesus; I believe what He did for me, and that He rose again on the third day! I want to share Him with others! I can't do that unless I practice my faith! I also need Him in my life! I need His presence! I thirst! I hunger for His word! I hunger for all that He can give me! I want to give back to Him! I want Him to know how much I love Him! I want to recognize His mother in my life! I want to continue to praise and worship Him, and not forget the sacrifice He made for me! I want to praise, adore and glorify Him! Without the Mass I cannot withstand the fiery darts of the evil one! I know I can stand strong and face anything when Jesus is with me and when I am standing in His grace! I will always be in love with Him, but not as much as when I am with Him and others, sharing in His Spirit! By His Body and Blood, I am saved in Christ's name.

ONE OF THE DEACONS GAVE A HOMILY RECENTLY, AND although now I cannot tell you exactly one word he said, I was listening. And his words inspired a thought of something I never really contemplated in full:

Jesus healed, as people of faith, pleaded to Him for cures. People reached out and were healed if they touched Christ.

We touch Christ at every Communion. I will now think of not only a healing physically, but spiritually in the forgiveness of sin and driving out the ever-present devil like an exorcism. Christ's physical healings were in the form of a release of demons or "confession" which required healing, like the forgiveness of sin.

Why I go to Mass now is for more awareness of actually touching Christ, initiating His healing power, physically and spiritually.

He's there to be touched "today" not a past of ~ 2000 years ago – a Miracle daily.

I WAS RAISED IN A CATHOLIC FAMILY. WE WENT TO MASS every Sunday as a family. That is what we did. When I got old enough to go to school, I went to a Catholic school. We went to Mass every morning before school started. The sisters at my elementary school told us that we were expected to go to Mass every morning. That is what we did.

When I got older, with the exception of a few years after college, I continued to go to Mass, at least every Sunday, because I CHOSE to. Now I am a wife, a mother, and a grandmother and I still choose to go to Mass.

Some of the reasons I go to Mass:

I know it to be the greatest of prayers which allows for the most intimate encounter with Jesus Christ.

The Mass is where I find the story of our salvation in Christ.

The Mass unites me with the heavenly liturgy. It is the closest I can get to Heaven on this earth, especially during the Consecration.

The Mass for me is also a sensory experience: the Eucharistic meal, the opulence of the vessels, the musical instruments and the voices of the choir united in praise, the glow of the candles, the ringing of the bells, the colors of the vestments worn by the celebrant for the particular season of the church year, the fragrance of the incense, and the absolute beauty of the church and its icons.

I participate in the Mass (liturgy of the Word and of the Eucharist) as a member of the Mystical Body of Christ.

In the liturgy of the word, I encounter the greatest story of love and redemption ever told.

The homily provides relatability and relevance which should spur me into action, sustained by the grace of the Holy Spirit.

St. Gregory the Great taught that a multitude of angels assist at the liturgy of the Eucharist. (Eucharist meaning Thanksgiving). Saint Gregory the Great, Dialogues, Book IV (1911), http://www.tertullian.org/fathers/gregory_04_dialogues_book4.htm

Imagine if we could witness this!!!

Christ died once for all of us. The Mass re-presents that sacrifice each time.

At the Last Supper, "While they were eating, Jesus took bread, said the blessing, broke it, and giving it to His disciples SAID, 'Take and eat; this is my body.' Then He took a cup, gave thanks, and gave it to them SAYING, 'Drink from it, all of you, for this is my blood of the covenant, which will be shed on behalf of many for the forgiveness of sins'" Matthew 26: 26-28.

Since Jesus is truth, why wouldn't we believe in the Real Presence? Do you realize what a gift this is?

You can't love what you don't know. Why would you stay away from the Mass?

I think of the angels gathering at the altar to join in on the Eucharistic sacrifice and celebration. While the angels can't partake of the Body and Blood of Christ, you can. Why wouldn't you?

One of the most memorable lines I ever heard in a sermon is that the Church "is not a Museum for Saints but rather a Hospital for Sinners." Mass provides some of the minor healing I need each week.

Any system left to itself will become more disordered over time. This is the concept of entropy, the Second Law of Thermodynamics. Think of a room that is so clean that it is spotless. Close the door, come back after a week, and don't be surprised to see a layer of dust upon all the previously immaculate surfaces.

Mass is a weekly dusting for the soul. Within the Gospel and Homily are weekly reminders, mini-lessons, in how we can become more Christ-like. Mass provides an opportunity to reflect upon how to live better.

We are inundated with messages to care for our physical and mental health. Health experts admonish us to exercise regularly and eat a healthy diet. Cognitive scientists coach us to engage our minds, practice gratitude, and connect with others. Consider though, how much more important it is to tend to our spiritual health.

One of the ways God has provided to build spiritual health is the Mass. We travel to church, express gratitude to the Lord, and connect with fellow believers. It is one of God's wonders that in caring for our spiritual health, we improve our overall health.

And yet, we all know there will come a time when our physical bodies will reach their end. Weekly Mass is a reminder of why and how we can prepare our souls for the journey that lies ahead.

THE MORE I STUDY ABOUT THE MASS, THE MORE I REALIZE that it is analogous structurally to a pyramid of sacred bricks. Each tier or layer of the pyramid is built upon the previous tier, and each and every brick is composed of a sacred truth(s) upon which our Faith exists. Thereby, missing any one brick (i.e., arriving late, not paying attention, or departing early) leaves a gap in the experience of the Mass.

I am in a learning curve about the Mass, using Bishop Barron's workbook on THE MASS as a guide to the wondrous content of each brick in the Mass. Attending daily Mass is an enriching experience. It is one of life's joys, as our priests point out so well and so often.

The Mass offers oral and visual experiences, and I find that much is missed if we choose to sit much behind the front of the nave. I no longer do so. There are too many distractions when I sit toward the back. This must also be the case for others.

✚

JESUS CLIMBED INTO MY ROCKY LITTLE BOAT WHEN I WAS A young mother and was questioning my faith. He brought His peace. He also put a great desire into my heart to know and love Him better. Always a church goer, I was a relatively new Catholic. My husband, a cradle Catholic, was active in our parishes even as we moved several times. Thankfully, we attended Sunday Mass and took advantage of Catholic formation in our parishes.

Little by little I have found that our Catholic Mass is the very best place to be close to Jesus. Thankfully, I can hear His Word in my own home each morning as I listen to the U.S. Conference of Catholic Bishops online. I can see His face as I cradle a grandchild or stand in line with strangers at the store. I can touch Him when I help with the homeless shelter or volunteer at a pregnancy help center. I know He listens as I speak to Him when I pray during the day and pray with my Rosary at night. He is in my little boat even if it is still sometimes rocked by the storms of life!

But when we walk into Mass…that is when we climb into HIS boat. He is there in everything…large and small. HE is there in the brothers and sisters who greet us. HIS Words reach us and grow us in the Scripture readings. HE loves us and teaches us during the homily. HE listens to us as we pray and sing together. HIS Love touches us in the most intimate way as HE comes to us in His Body and Blood at Communion! He invites us to take His Peace with us when we step back onto the shore and head to our own little boats and wherever they take us. He comes with us!

I go to Mass to know Jesus. I go to Mass to be with Jesus because I love Him and because He loves us!

✚

I GO TO MASS TO WORSHIP GOD, MY FATHER AND JESUS, MY brother, both of whom I love very much. I gaze with delight, gratitude, and love at Jesus in the Eucharist and softly utter words of praise and thanksgiving. I thank God for the many blessings he has provided me, my family, relatives, and friends. I praise God because He is worthy of my adoration and love, and I ask Him to help me honor Him in all that I do.

As the priest raises the host during the consecration, I utter words of praise and love, and I tell Jesus that I believe He is present and to help my unbelief. Sometimes, when I gaze at Jesus in the Eucharist, I sense that I am on holy ground. Like Moses before the burning bush, I hear my Father, God saying, "take off your shoes, you are walking on holy ground."

I also worship God in the songs we sing during Mass. As I sing, I feel that I am talking directly to Jesus through the words of the song. In the silence after communion, I hear Jesus telling me how much He loves me and that He has His hand on my back to guide and support me.

As I leave Mass, I again express my gratitude to Jesus for all He has done for me, my family, relatives, and friends.

I GO TO CHURCH TO ADORE OUR LORD, WHO HUMBLES Himself daily in every Catholic Church all over the world, to be with us. When I was in high school and college, I would often stop to visit the school chapel on my way in or out of classes. I did not really understand that Christ was present, not in the intellectual sense anyway, but I was amazed at how my anxieties would fall like broken shackles when I knelt in prayer before the tabernacle. Later, when I traveled to Italy on a pilgrimage to see the Shroud of Turin, I remember being in awe of being so close to something that had actually touched Jesus Christ. But as the priest reminded us during the homily at Mass that day, we are even closer to our Lord every time we receive the Eucharist, as we are consuming the true body of Christ within us.

I go to Church because it is my place of refuge, my source of hope. When I am struggling with a decision or anxious about something, I will stop into a Catholic Church and light a candle, praying for a sick relative, for a special intention, or to discern God's will. After my parents and other loved ones passed away, it was a place of solace. I would enter a church and feel God's loving presence; reassuring me I was not alone, and that those whom I have loved and lost were with at peace and with Christ.

For years, I prayed to have a family. And now that God has answered my prayers beyond anything I could have imagined, I go to Church in thanksgiving, and to pray for guidance to raise the family He has given me. I want my children to realize that God has blessed us abundantly, and that He should be the center of their lives. I go to Church and thank Him for His countless blessings and to pray for His help to instill a faith in them that will reunite us all to Christ in Heaven.

I go to Church to ask for forgiveness, through the sacrament of Reconciliation, and when kneeling before Christ in the Eucharist. I often resist, rather than embrace the Cross, succumbing to anxiety and impatience, and falling into the same selfish sins. I think of the humility of the Blessed Mother, patiently accepting her difficult circumstances, selflessly loving and serving her family while trusting the will of God. How unlike I am to her! During Confession, or before the tabernacle, I pray to God for His forgiveness and help to be more like the Blessed Mother when raising my children.

The world draws me in with constant distractions, urging me to a life of busyness, comfort and pleasure. But through it all, a quiet voice calls me to the place where Christ is, the Source of true joy, hope and love. My soul hears the Word of God and recognizes the Wisdom that surpasses all understanding. So, I go to church, our Catholic Church, to hear the Truth, and to be with God, who has so lovingly availed Himself to us in every Tabernacle of the world.

I GO TO MASS BECAUSE I AM IN LOVE WITH GOD AND HE IS IN love with me. As with all lovers we want to be near each other and to see each other as much as possible. I am the closest to God when I am at Mass and when I receive Him in Holy Communion.

When I receive Communion, I love the thought that I am holding Jesus in my hand; just as Mary and Joseph held Him when He was born. I love knowing Jesus is with me and becomes a part of me whenever I receive Him. I love talking to God and sharing my joys, sorrows, and decisions. I love knowing He always listens and gives me what He thinks is best.

God is love and He is so good to me. I go to Mass to honor and show Him my love for Him.

I GO TO MASS TO BE CLOSER TO JESUS. THE SACRAMENT OF Holy Communion, the Eucharist, is truly the Body and Blood, Soul and Divinity of Jesus Christ, our Savior, our Redeemer. Jesus paid a terrible price, through His passion and death on the cross, so that we might have eternal life with Him forever in Heaven. I admit there have been times in my life where I may have taken the opportunity to attend Mass for granted, but when I read about Juan Diego walking fifteen miles three times a week to attend Mass, I am humbled by the great love and sacrifice of the saints. All I have to do is drive or walk a short distance to attend Mass without fear of being arrested, imprisoned or put to death for doing so. Because Jesus said,

"Do this in remembrance of Me," when He instituted the Eucharist at the Last Supper, it is with gratitude that I attend Mass. It isn't that I have to attend Mass; it is that I am blessed to be able to attend Mass.

Remembering the Stations of the Cross reminds me of the Passion of Christ and all He had to endure to give us this greatest treasure - Himself offered as the sacrificial lamb and serving as the priest also to give us the gift of eternal life with Him forever in Heaven. And why? Why did Jesus suffer so? He suffered out of His great love for us - sinners though we are. Yet, He humbled himself so that we might have life with Him. Because I desire to be humble, to be obedient to God as He showed us, I long to participate at Mass. Because He loved us so much and I desire to love Him in return, that is why I go to Mass.

Here is an interesting true story of an incident that occurred one time when I made what I believed to be a very small sacrifice to attend Sunday Mass while on a business trip in California. There was quite an exciting event planned at the fancy, upscale hotel where I was staying and where my company was participating as a service vendor for law firms at a convention. Apparently, the President of the United States (this was many years before 9/11) was presenting an award to a famous actor for his work encouraging children and other citizens in physical fitness. Many movie stars were attending the event that was to be held on this particular Saturday evening. My boss informed us that we were all invited to meet for cocktails at 5:00 pm in the lounge and watch the movie stars as they walked by in their evening apparel to the event. We finished work in the early afternoon and my coworkers and I headed back to our rooms. My boss told me that I had to be ready to receive equipment that was arriving early Sunday morning. I was in charge of making sure all the equipment was delivered, set-up and working prior to the convention. I realized that Sunday morning and afternoon would be fully booked with duties for my job. I soon realized that the best time for me to attend Mass was at 5:00 pm that Saturday evening.   I planned to take a cab to the hotel so as not to be late, and then walk back to the hotel since it was a short distance away. I realized also that this meant I would miss the cocktail gathering and watching the movie stars as they walked by the lounge on their way to the event. Oh well, I thought, maybe I'll get back in time to see a few of the stars, but I did not want to skip Mass. In my mind, Mass was not just something I was obligated to do, but a very holy sacrament that I was blessed to be a part of. Long ago, my teacher, a Catholic nun, taught me that Jesus was my best friend. How could I stand up my best friend for movie stars that didn't even know me? I went to Mass with no regrets.

As I walked back after Mass, I enjoyed the walk down the beautiful Los Angeles street and I felt content and peaceful. Figuring my coworkers might still be at the lounge, I thought I would check. As I walked by the lounge, I spotted my coworkers. They were very excited and exclaimed that I had missed everything. They stated names of all the numerous stars they had seen and described their beautiful attire, diamond earrings and all. Then they asked me, "Where were you?" I replied that I had gone to Mass nearby. My answer caused them to explode with laughter. One gentleman nearly choked as he almost spit out his cocktail.   "What!" he exclaimed, "You missed seeing the stars to go to church?" and he convulsed in laughter. The other three coworkers joined in the laughter, too. Honestly, their reaction did not surprise nor upset me.   However, then my boss started to make dinner plans, and this I was not prepared for, she excluded me from the invitation to dine with her and my coworkers. I think she feared I would not be fun to hang out with. At first, I was a little disappointed, but then I just told myself to make the best of it. After all, I was in a lovely hotel with plenty of places to eat. I got dressed up in my fanciest dress suit and went to the elevator. In the elevator, I met the music manager of the band that was playing at the event as entertainment for the stars. I asked the manager if she thought I could sit in the back and watch the show. We exited the elevator and the manager walked with me towards the doors to the event, she showed me a security guard and told me that I should check with him. I repeated my question to the security guard. (Remember this was many years before 9/11). He pointed to a table in the back and said the secret service men had been sitting at that table. As soon as they had finished leaving the hotel with the President, I could sit at the empty table.

When I sat down at the table, a waiter, who I had met earlier when I was setting up for work, recognized me and served me dessert with champagne. I got there just in time to hear the band perform. I saw the stars all sitting nearby at tables around me. I even got to shake hands with the Master of Ceremonies, a famous actor, as he said goodbye to departing guests. Back in my hotel room, my boss called me to tell me I hadn't missed anything, dinner was boring she said. Then she asked me about my evening. I told her and she was so excited she made me repeat it again! She told the coworkers about it the next day and had me repeat my story again. After that, she never excluded me from the outings or dinners.

I never expected such a treat here on earth for going to Mass. Giving up the cocktail hour to attend Mass was a minuscule sacrifice. Jesus is the Way, the Truth, and the Life. I'll choose Jesus every day whether in time of joy or tribulation. I tell my children and students, never expect a reward for going to church, you have already received the most precious sacrament – Jesus, truly present in the Eucharist.

✞

SOMETIMES, MASS CAN SEEM LIKE JUST ANOTHER THING TO DO. Just another thing on our schedule. Often, it can seem like we're not really getting anything out of it.

That thought couldn't be more wrong.

All over the world, throughout different parts of history, people have fought and died to be free to worship God. We worship every time we go to Mass. People have struggled to be able to read the Bible. We do that every time we go to Mass. Jesus Himself came down from Heaven, suffered, and died for us, so that we could be with Him. He comes to us in the Eucharist every time we go to Mass.

We receive God's Word, and *Himself*, when we go to Mass. We cannot claim that we get nothing out of it.

And yet, there is even *more* to the Mass than that. Even more to it than what we get out of it.

When we go to Mass, we worship God.

That is the reason. The *purpose* of going to Mass. We aren't there simply to "get something out of it"—in fact, that thought alone shows how self-centered we can be. We aren't there to worship us. We are there to worship God, because He deserves our worship. We are not only there to receive Him— we are there to give ourselves to Him, too.

So, whenever we think that we're "not getting anything out of going to Mass," it's important for us to remind ourselves— we are receiving *so much*, and, more importantly, we're not just there to receive.

We are there to worship Him.

IT TOOK ME AWHILE TO RESPOND TO YOUR QUESTION ABOUT what the Mass means to me because it is so hard to express in words something so special.

I go to Mass because there I meet Jesus in person. It is a living, loving encounter with Him, where He fills in my heart of joy. He fills in those dark places of pain, sadness, and loneliness, much of which stems from the loss of my dad in 2020, giving me peace. The presence of Jesus fortifies and renews my body and soul to face another week. It is also comforting to hear through the voice of the priest at Mass, the messages that Jesus wants us to hear. Many times it is as if He is talking with us directly.

EVER SINCE I WAS A YOUNG ALTAR BOY, THERE HAS BEEN something very special to me about the Mass. After my First Communion at the age of eight, a distant cousin asked me to join him as an altar boy. I was reluctant at first, but after he showed me the ropes during that first Mass, there was something special that I felt. I found myself captivated by the movements of the priest during the Mass, especially during that high point of the Mass, the Consecration. Altar boys would kneel in front of the altar in those days, with our backs to the congregation, so it was impossible not to keep my eyes fixated on the priest, as he raised the host and then the chalice. Each time when it was my turn to ring the bells at each designated moment, there was something special that I felt. It was as if nobody else was in that church except me, the priest, and Jesus in the form of bread and wine. I have read that St. John Chrysostom once said that angels surround the priest and the altar at that special moment of Consecration. I often think of that and realize that special moment is as close to Heaven as we can be on earth.

Even today, after nearly fifty years as an altar boy, I still have that same feeling as an adult, being drawn to that special moment of the Mass, when Jesus' presence in the form of bread and wine culminates in the greatest prayer of the Church. Each week, I look forward to going to Mass, as it brings me a rejuvenation, a sense of my lowliness as a sinner, but also the hope and promise from Jesus himself, that he will feed us and make us one with him. I see the Mass as my opportunity to give back to Jesus praise and thanksgiving for all the ways that He has blessed me, but in that opportunity of thanking Him, he again gives me all that I could ever desire in His gift to me of Himself, coming to me and making me one with Him.

I GO TO MASS BECAUSE I LOVE JESUS!! I ALSO GO TO MASS because I don't want to go to hell. I want to be ready when I die to see Jesus in Heaven. Jesus died to save our souls. Jesus told us to celebrate the Mass.

The Holy Spirit

Four Lasting Considerations in Life: Death, Judgment, Heaven and Hell

Therefore, bear in mind that I will strive to be in Heaven in the next life and not to the everlasting fire in Hell. I think about my immortal soul because someday I will die. We all end this way. Therefore, I bear in mind that I strive for Heaven in the next life and not the everlasting fire in Hell.

How will this be accomplished? I try to go to Mass every day, if possible, because the graces, blessing and favors granted to those who assist at the Divine Sacrifice devoutly are beyond comprehension; it is essential for our salvation. It's the greatest means for attaining our salvation.

Here is Jesus' Real Presence on the altar waiting to be received by us. It is Jesus' Body, Blood, Soul and Divinity. He is humbling Himself to come to us. He shuts Himself in the tabernacle in the form of Bread so that He can be found by everyone that seeks Him. He is a "Prisoner of Love."

Mass brings about the actual Sacrifice of Calvary, the actual Passion, Death and Resurrection of Christ who died for us for our salvation. Through the Crucifixion of Christ and His Resurrection, God the Father reconciled with us. Before the Crucifixion, Heaven was closed due to the sin committed by our first parents, Adam and Eve, who committed the Sin of Pride.

Therefore, we must remember then that in the Holy Sacrifice of the Mass, Jesus Christ offers Himself to His Father, adoring Him and petitioning Him on behalf of His Church, of men His brothers (we) and all the poor sinners. At this point the work of our redemption is accomplished.

Now maybe the reason we neglect to attend Mass is because most of us lost the sense of Sacredness of the Mass. The modern world has taken from us our belief in the Real Presence, and some of us have fallen in love with the pleasures of the world against which Christ warned us. We no longer believe in the reality of Satan and his power as the Prince of this material world.

The Holy Sacrifice of the Mass is the same as that of the Cross, which was offered once on Calvary on Good Friday. The only difference is that, when Jesus Christ offered Himself on Calvary, the Sacrifice was visible; that is to say, Jesus Christ was seen with the bodily eyes, being offered to God, His Father, by the hands of His executioners, and shedding of His Blood. It means that the Blood came forth from His veins and was seen flowing down upon the ground. But in the Holy Mass, Jesus Christ offers Himself to His Father in an invisible and bloodless manner.

I hope and pray that you ask the Holy Spirit to guide you in how to love your God Jesus through Mary. I will be with you always in prayers to help you find and love Jesus again in your lifetime.

I go to Mass because of God the Father, Jesus in the Eucharist, the Holy Spirit, the angels and saints, His Church both in Heaven and on Earth. Why?

God the Father, because He said to Moses and Aaron to make it a perpetual institution.

Jesus Christ, because He said, "Amen, amen, I say to you, it was not Moses who gave the bread from Heaven; my Father gives you the true bread from Heaven. For the bread of God is that which comes down from Heaven and gives life to the world. I am the bread of life; whoever comes to me will never hunger, and whoever believes in me will never thirst. But I told you that although you have seen [me], you do not believe." I don't want to be like the disciples who left because they were shocked and thought what He said was too hard to believe.

The Holy Spirit, because He is an Advocate. I always need one.

The angels and His saints, because they never cease to intercede for us and who knows, they just might be our family, maybe our grandparents, even our parents or children who are in Heaven.

The members of the church because they have become my community, some more like family. I get to partake in a banquet and, if you know me, food is my love language. Except, this is the most important meal with a few hundred friends!

Last but not least, I get to worship as the Father had prescribed in the Old Testament, I even get to be with my friends and family whether they are in Heaven or on earth, kneel in worship which the angels can't do, and be most intimate with Jesus by being one with Him: Body, Blood, Soul and Divinity!

"Why wouldn't I go to Mass?" is the more important question!

WHY DO I GO TO MASS? OF COURSE, THE THIRD Commandment requires it.

Obviously, that's not the only reason. My story…

I went to Sunday/Holy Day Masses with my parents for as long back as I can remember. Then I attended Catholic grade school and high school - the Baltimore Catechism drilled into me at a young age. Initially my attention span at Mass was short. But as I grew older, gradually my mindset at Mass changed. Somewhere along the line, I came to realize and started paying attention to the Holy Spirit whispering to me - helping me discern right from wrong, even in the smallest of things. Attending Mass started making sense.

Today, upon entering the church and kneeling before Mass, I start a prayer. It's the same every time: I offer this Mass in Praise, Thanksgiving, and Petition. In **Praise** of my God's might and right; in **Thanksgiving** for all the gifts and blessings He has bestowed on me throughout my life (my parents, my wife, my children, my health, sending His Son to show us how to save ourselves, etc.); and in **Petition**, I pray for something different at every Mass, (the end to gun violence in our cities, help for latest hurricane and fire victims, change in the thinking of those people who believe abortion is okay, etc.). Of course, near the end of Mass, I have the privilege of receiving Our Lord at Communion. What can be better than that?!

My mind still wanders at times, but it is, little by little, improving.

I GO TO MASS BECAUSE:

- The God Who Is, the God Who Was and the God Who Ever Will Be asked me to.
- The Father who created all that is, all that was and all that ever will be invited me to a Sunday meal at His house.
- The Holy Spirit who breathed life into me and sustains me in all that I do is waiting to rejoice with me.
- Jesus who suffered and died on the cross to redeem me has offered to nourish me and strengthen me for the coming week.
- The almighty God of all the universe is waiting to spend an hour with me each week.
- Because I need to.

I FEEL THE REASON I COME TO MASS IS FOR THE PURPOSE OF resting with God. Through the sacraments, community, and most importantly the celebration of the Mass, we are united as people with a common goal: to praise, worship, and love our Father and support each other in relationship with Him and with others.

I don't think I "got" this until recently though. It was the constant yearning to know, love, and serve Him that makes it all come together.

That is an individual decision, a journey, and something that only the Holy Spirit and our free will can fulfill. It begins as a small seed through the sacrament of Baptism and grows through the other sacramental graces. All these steps lead us to the desire to know Him and love Him even more.

I did want to include that many of the church's ministries/outreaches helped me in hearing His call. I began a long time ago with Renew (an at-home bible study). That then led me to many other bible studies and faith sharing groups. A parishioner also took me under her wing during the pandemic and taught me all about salvation history. What a life changing gift that was! Lastly, I am lucky enough to be in a Quad with a beautiful group of women of all ages. These are all things going on at Saint Mary's and the many people that make it so wonderful.

The church and its people are always there to support and encourage us, but they cannot be our Savior. Only God can do that. And where better to find Him but in the Mass?

As a Catholic I respond to Mary as the Mother of God. The profound love I have for her equals no other! I have found in her goodness that I exist, her tender mercies, and how she loves me through her Son Jesus Christ. I believe that without Mary we would be incomplete. God has chosen her to help us redeem the world. I am grateful for her sacred and immaculate heart. I am earnest in my desire to help her overcome the evils of this world. I give her my attention and respect as you would give your mother. I am totally willing to listen to her for guidance as I make my way through the day, trusting her spouse, the Holy Spirit. Amen.

I go to Mass because I have an obligation to keep holy one day in seven, and going to Mass substantially fulfills that obligation.

I go to Mass to worship, honor, and praise God and to

thank Him for the many blessings He has bestowed upon me and my family.

I go to Mass to ask God for His forgiveness and for His continued help to avoid evil and to obey His commandments.

I go to Mass to ask for wisdom and insight to better know Him and to understand what He wants of me.

I go to Mass to commemorate the sacrifice of the Lamb of God who takes away the sins of the world.

I go to Mass to eat His body and drink His blood which is essential to sustain my quest for eternal life.

I go to Mass to strengthen my faith which provides meaning for my existence, order in my life, and hope for my future. Without these gifts, nothingness becomes a reality and life becomes meaningless.

Sexual Abuse

"Father, forgive them; for they know not what they do."

— *LUKE 23:34*

Some of the stories provided by our parishioners speak of struggles. The following stories speak specifically to the painful tragedy of sexual abuse both by Church leaders and within families.

We include these stories to honor those who struggle and to speak lovingly to those who have come forward with their stories, to those who are still on the edges of trust, to those who struggle because of the weaknesses and failures of the humans who make up our Church, to those who pray for the abused and the abuser. All are welcome here.

The sexual abuse scandal in the Catholic Church has brought a deep sorrow to our bishops, priests, staff, as well as the lay faithful. Our prayers for hope and healing go out to all victims/survivors of sexual abuse, regardless of the source of their abuse.

The Parish of St Mary of Sorrows and the Diocese of Arlington's Office of Victim Assistance seek to extend the loving compassion of Christ to all victims/survivors of any sexual abuse throughout their healing process.

St. Mary of Sorrows:
contactus@stmaryofsorrows.org
(703) 978-4141

Office of Victim Assistance:
200 North Glebe Road, Suite 605, Arlington, VA
22203
victimassistance@arlingtondiocese.org
(703) 841-2530

"We have listened to many people suffering from the agony of abuse, and endeavor to walk with each person on this painful journey towards healing and wholeness through and with Jesus Christ."

> — DR. FRANK MONCHER, VICTIM
> ASSISTANCE COORDINATOR,
> ARLINGTON DIOCESE

"In the end, we are not Catholics because our leaders are flawless, but because we find the claims of Catholicism both compelling and beautiful. We are Catholics because the Church speaks of the Trinitarian God whose very nature is love; of Jesus the Lord, crucified and risen from the dead; of the Holy Spirit, who inspires the followers of Christ up and down the ages; of the sacraments, which convey the Christ-life to us; and of the saints, who are our friends in the spiritual order. This is the treasure; this is why we stay."

— BISHOP ROBERT BARRON

My wife and I attend Mass in person every weekend at St Mary of Sorrows and online almost every day at the Loretto Abbey web site. We do so because we were both raised in faithfully practicing Catholic families. It's almost a habit we developed, grew up with and is now just ingrained in our daily lives.

But, it's far more than just a routine we practice. We attend Mass because it's a form of spiritual strength and sustenance that we feel gives us a "daily shot in the soul" to help get through the challenges we all face in our lives. It's also an hour or so when we're just able to put aside the issues and challenges of "the world" and concentrate instead on what's really important, i.e., "love of God and the salvation of our immortal souls."

Though you didn't ask for it, I'm going to say why I think many Catholics no longer attend Mass.

1 - The church's handling of the Priests' abuse of young children was poor and criminal in many areas. This has left a really bad feeling for a lot of formerly good Catholics who have fallen away from attending Mass because they no longer believe in the honesty and forth righteousness of the priestly community.

2 - The performance of the top leadership in the Church today. The Cardinal McCarrick case is a prime example, but there are many others and that has really turned people off.

It's akin to the political leadership we have in this country today.

I'll leave it there. Thanks for the opportunity to share my thoughts with you. God Bless.

Pain. Fear. Shame. Isolation. Betrayal. Destruction of the ideas of family, of mother and father, of home. Destruction of the concept of safety. Crushing the idea of a God who cares at all, loves at all. Church as a dangerous place to be. The belief that there is a deep black hole where one's soul should be.

Hopelessness. Despair.

Whether one is six or ten or sixteen, sexual abuse shatters faith, often even before it can become real.

Mass becomes a place of confusion, dread. It becomes utter hypocrisy. A lie which feeds the shame.

Or so it seems.

But someone puts their hands on your shoulders and turns you to face Our Eucharistic Lord. They take you by the hand and lead you to Confession, to His mercy and grace. They help you begin, just begin, to hear the love Our Lord has for you. They help you consider the possibility. By being trustworthy, they allow you the place to begin to trust God…a little bit.

They tell you…over and over again…that the Mass is the opposite of everything you knew. And they are right.

Pain becomes comfort. Fear becomes quiet confidence. Shame becomes mercy. Isolation becomes communion. Family, Mother, Father become places of safety instead of danger. Betrayal becomes being wrapped in a protective embrace. Hope and love replace the emptiness of abuse.

There continue to be stumbles, but there are those, guided by God's love, who are a gentle presence while you regain your footing, trust enough to again open your eyes.

And you go to Mass. In the chaos of the world, you go to Him. In the midst of confusion, you go to the One who is constant. You go to Love Incarnate.

Mass promotes healing. Mass helps restore faith. With our cooperation, He transforms us.

ONE OF THE REASONS I ATTEND MASS REGULARLY IS BECAUSE I feel it is my duty and obligation as a Roman Catholic to do so. This is the way I was raised as a Catholic and I feel it is the right thing to do in order to call myself a Catholic. Mass also brings me peace knowing that I can "lay my cards on the table," so to speak, and ask for guidance with the challenges ahead. Mass is also a good time to thank God for everything that has been provided to me over time and acknowledge the fact that He helped me along the way. It is a great time to pray too.

That being said, it does present some challenges. I have become so discouraged with the clergy sex abuse issues that have taken place and it is hard for me to accept the acknowledgement from the clergy and the apologies. I know there are good and great priests in the Church, but this just keeps going on with no end in sight.

I have found it very hard to hear the word and wonder what it is supposed to mean coming from someone who may be an offender. Thank God I am old school and hold on to my beliefs a lot deeper than some people today.

It is also hard being challenged by your own adult children and trying to justify the need for going to church. I respond the best I can and lead by example as a Jesuit Priest counseled me to do at a retreat. I would rather have an ongoing relationship with my family than to have Sunday Mass attendance be a wedge in that relationship.

✠

For so long I went to Mass because I was "supposed" to, and it was very important that I did what looked right even if it was solely for appearances. I was hiding in plain sight... hiding from God.

At age seven, trying to figure how to survive in my world filled with sexual abuse, I decided that God was extraordinarily angry with me, and I needed to hide from Him. The brain of a child trying to make sense of a world that makes no sense can lead one to wrong conclusions; conclusions that are extraordinarily hard to leave behind even as an adult.

Once I found myself in an environment in which I felt safe, trust had become a possibility. With the Lord's gentle, loving nudges and the opportunities He created for me, and the people He put in my life who could help me shed those ideas ingrained in my mind and heart after so very many decades, trust has become more than a possibility.

With the Lord's grace I have been able to walk, or sometimes stumble, through the pain towards healing. Is it easy? Never. I fall often. It seems that I must learn to trust over and over again. But I am learning that God has faith in me even when my faith...in me or Him...falters.

What does all of this have to do with going to Mass? Everything. When I am feeling confident, I can go and celebrate and praise and honor and adore. When I am feeling shaky...or I am feeling so very broken...I can go and be in His Presence, receive Him into my broken body. I can go and gain strength, sometimes the strength I need to forgive others, sometimes the strength I need to forgive myself, sometimes the strength I need to put one foot in front of the other or breathe or just hold on.

Each time I gain the same thing: Him, and each time I gain something different because each time I go I am different. He is the constant that I lacked as a child and lacked as an adult with a child's world view.

Each time I go to Mass, regardless of my state of being, He is there waiting for me, so delighted that I have come, so ready to offer Himself to me. Each time I go I can give Him whoever I am that day, whatever the struggles are, whatever the joys are, whatever the confusion is, and He lovingly takes me in His arms and reminds me that He finds me precious.

Once upon a time I could only say the first part of the prayer…"Lord, I am not worthy that you should enter under my roof…" I was so good at the "unworthy" part. With time, His grace, and the blessings He has placed in my life, I can now actually say, and pray, the rest of it, "but only say the word and my soul shall be healed."

For all those who have suffered the trauma of child sexual abuse, for all those who know someone who was abused, for all those appalled by, hurt by, the sexual abuse scandals within the Church, the way to healing is through the sacraments, through the Mass, through all that Our Lord has given us to help us and protect us in a world that does not always seem to make sense.

Young People

"Guard what has been entrusted to you."

— *1 TIM 6:20*

I would like to recommend, in particular, daily or frequent Mass to all young Catholics. Why? Because we all know that teenagers are in the formative time of their lives. Many of us are fraught with anxiety and ignorance. The Mass is the answer to all of your problems. Some of the benefits I have noticed are better focus and a better mood throughout the day. When I start my morning with praying to God my day is a better one.

Mass is the climax of the day. Daily or frequent Mass is an easy way to Heaven. Many do not have the opportunity; so, if you are blessed with the opportunity, do not waste it. Without daily Mass, I know that my teenage life would be much worse. Without God we are lost.

ALTHOUGH I'M ONLY A TEENAGER, I STILL ENJOY AND LOOK forward to going to Mass every Sunday. I look forward to going to Mass because I love being able to hear the Gospels, readings, and the homily and to then be able to, if I concentrate, hear God speaking to me, telling me what it is that He wants me to do this week to be able to grow closer to Him and to fulfill my part in His plan. I know that it is God speaking to me when I hear something said at Mass or a thought comes out of nowhere, and I get this overjoyed, bubbly feeling in my chest, in my heart. I get that feeling of revelation, and I finally understand what was said or what I just "heard."

I sometimes feel lost, confused, worried, and overwhelmed wondering what it is that I am supposed to do to help make this big world a better place, and what I need to do, as a young person, to use my gifts and talents and things that God has blessed me with to be a servant of Him and to be a good person. What I have learned that is if I pray and pay attention at Mass, God will tell me what I need to do. He will actually help me to make these decisions that were so hard to make before.

I've realized that in going to Mass and listening to God, I don't have to be scared and stressed and worried and confused, God will always be with me and He will help me. I do not have to go at it alone. That is why I go to Mass.

FOR ME, MASS IS A SAFE PLACE FILLED WITH HOPE, LOVE, AND faith. It is not just a building, but a home where I belong. Before every service, I am greeted with kind, welcoming faces that bring me into a good mood. I know that when I come to Mass contentment and glee will wash over me. It does not matter how disappointed, upset, or irritated I am because being in the presence of Jesus makes everything vanish. Mass gives me the opportunity to praise and give thanks to God, who loved me first. I go to Mass because of the joy I feel being able to worship and share my faith with others.

SOME THINGS ARE ONLY AVAILABLE AT ONE PLACE. SOME stores have exclusive items and are the reason shoppers come back over and over again. Likewise, there is only one place where I can receive the Eucharist, attend Adoration, celebrate Mass, and discuss my faith freely at SMOS Youth Group. The best memories I have of church are at the youth group and at "Time Out Tuesday" after school. Not only is it fun, it helps me to become more confident in sharing my faith outside of the parish.

Senior Citizens

"That my joy may be in you, and that your joy may be full."

— JOHN 15:11

I am now 78 years old and have been going to daily Mass, if somewhat irregularly, since I was in high school. In fact, one of my most vivid memories of that comes from my junior year in high school. I had decided to get up early and go to Mass before school for Lent. Well, one morning that must have left me quite sleepy and I dozed off during Chemistry class. At some point I was awakened by Brother William saying loudly, "Mister, the door is OPEN and it swings OUT." Needless to say, that kept me awake for the rest of class! I was able to attend and serve daily Mass for a priest friend during college. In grad school, I used to attend the daily Mass held in an all-purpose room on campus and that's where I met my wife. I found a church near work in D.C. where I went to noon Mass and ended up as a lector there for over 25 years. Since retirement, I have done the same thing at St. Mary's.

The question of why we attend Mass is an excellent one. I wish I could say that it is because I am especially devout; I am not. Alas, I don't find that the Mass automatically absorbs all my attention, as it should. I don't walk away from Mass and Communion on a wonderful high, much less levitate like St. Thomas Aquinas. Basically, the reason I attend is that, despite my lack of devotion, a small voice tells me it is what I should do, and most of the time I am able to follow that voice; the reasons for that I leave to God.

I regularly struggle to be devout and to pay attention to the incredible meaning of the Mass and insert myself into that meaning, but I regularly find my attention wandering off into the "La-La Land" of whatever is going on in my life or coming up during the day.

The disturbing thought occasionally hits me how often I receive Jesus in the Eucharist and then find my mind wandering off, and how it's like inviting Him into my house and then leaving Him sitting while I head off to my office to do whatever is pressing for the day. I am consoled by the thought that just as it is better to have loved and lost than never loved at all, it is better to have shown up and given whatever attention and devotion I can muster than never show up at all.

See you in Church.

Why do I go to daily Mass? Because that is where HE is.

The longer answer is that at my age I shall be seeing him soon - I'm trying to be more ready. I also have a large family and there is always at least one needing prayer or a trip to Lourdes.

As I find myself in my 90th year, I can look back and say that I was pointed in the right direction of going to Mass on Sundays and Holy Days of Obligation by two remarkable parents and the good sisters of the Immaculate Heart of Mary. Both my parents and the sisters set me on the right path at a very early age. Now I'm strengthened by the good example of a wife of 64 years to help me continue to be focused on the right path.

That's the easy answer. Now, as my time draws to a close, I find that the Baltimore Catechism provides the answer on its first page. "Why did God make me?" The Celebration of the Mass brings me nearer to God, and gives me the best opportunity to get to know Him, to love Him, to believe in Him, to hope in Him, to listen to Him, and to serve Him.

God's love to all hands!

I GO TO CHURCH BECAUSE IT HELPS ME ACQUIRE AND MAINTAIN a sense of happiness.

I am a senior citizen who is always busy. I try to live in harmony with nature, people, and my immediate community. I also love to travel.

Going to church enables me to spend time in prayer, thanking God for all His blessings!

I have been through a high degree of adversity. The Lord has always been there for me.

St. Mary of Sorrows Church is such a beautiful place of worship. It inspires me to meditate during the Mass.

I truly <u>need</u> to participate in the Mass. As a Catholic woman of faith, the least I could do is to stop what I'm doing, and attend an hour Mass on a weekly basis.

So, God willing, I am determined to go to Mass weekly. I have found happiness in doing so.

THREE YEARS AGO, AT 85 YEARS ON THE PLANET AND AS A "minimalist Catholic," I awakened to what it's all about, and began going to daily Mass (among other things).

And that's why I go to Mass on Sunday as well as every day that I can.

MY THREE OLDER SISTERS AND I WERE RAISED BY POLISH immigrants who did become U.S. citizens. They had a strong commitment to church and Mass. This was passed on to all of us without any questions.

We all attended parochial school for nine years and fully participated in our church's services. When we weren't in school (summer), we attended with our parents.

Before I was eligible for First Communion, I remember always crying when people went up to the altar rail to receive Communion and I couldn't. I longed for that moment. Needless to say, my First Communion was extremely important to me and I was very happy.

I've never missed Mass intentionally and I am now in my late 70's. Going to church and attending Mass on Sundays or any day is a desire and not an obligation. I attend Mass even when on vacation and have attended in other U.S. states, Europe and South America. Although I feel God's presence with me all the time, I especially feel it when I go to His house and receive Communion.

The pandemic brought home the reality of how I took for granted the easy availability of attending Mass and receiving Communion. When Masses needed to be halted, I watched on EWTN and the livestream. That was better than nothing. But, coming into the Parish Center to pray before the Crucifix and then, thankfully, the Exposition of the Host, made the impact of not having Mass/Communion emotional. I thought of all the people of different nations who don't have easy access as I did.

Now, it was the same for me.

I love the Mass, the beautiful rituals, the prayers, songs and finally the Consecration. There is a difference in the atmosphere after the Consecration. Receiving Jesus sustains me in my Earthly journey. I would never give that gift away.

WHEN ASKED TO CONSIDER WRITING "WHY DO I GO TO Mass?" it initially provided me pause, reflection, and some introspection. On the one hand, my Catholic upbringing certainly formed a strong basis for Mass attendance on every Sunday and Holy Day of Obligation. Growing up in the 1950's and 1960's in a strong Catholic household, reinforced by 12 years of Catholic schooling, attending Mass on Sundays and Holy Days of Obligation, was an unquestioned weekly practice. More than that, it was a seed that was sprouted and nurtured through the exceptional example of parents, teachers, and clergy.

Now, blessedly enjoying the grace of my senior years, I find that the practice of attending Mass is a manifestation of who I am and an acknowledgement of my Catholic faith. While giving glory, praise, and thanks for the gift of the Eucharist, I am in a community of people who pray for our unique individual challenges and communal and societal needs, as well as for our spiritual well-being and growth. I value hearing and understanding the Word of God through the scriptural readings and the Gospel. I challenge myself to commit to that Word. Most importantly, reliving the ultimate sacrifice of Jesus Christ, I have the awesome opportunity to receive His true Body and Blood which strengthens me in ways I may not even realize.

I sometimes read of many who, at one point or another, moved away from this practice. It could be that the seed that germinated so many years ago encountered a disruption to grow and thrive. Perhaps some other circumstances presented themselves as a spiritual challenge unique to that individual leading, to among other decisions, to forego Mass attendance. Societal shifts and challenges, some within the church itself, have taken their tolls. Yet, for those who find themselves in these circumstances, we often hear of instances whereby returning to the practice of Mass attendance makes them even more appreciative of the grace that Mass brings. Those who return to the practice after an absence are worthy spiritual role models for all.

And though I attend Mass regularly, I must never forget to fully appreciate and embrace the experience in entirety. Maybe a good practice would be to ask myself, "Why Am I Attending Mass Today?" every time I am walking from the parking lot to the church.

A Return to Faith

"I thirst."

— JOHN 19:28

I go to Mass because it is the door to understanding my purpose.

It takes great courage to believe in the truths of our Catholic faith. Our faith is not an easy undertaking, but rather a direct challenge to the heart that wants to sense faith and to the intellect that demands to know it. Both can be rebuffed. Discouragement is easy, leading one to either drift away to something else - or nothing else – or to be reduced to sterile compliance with rites without purpose.

For too many years I was in the latter category, a Catholic wanderer of sorts, and worse I was slowly creeping toward atheism. Our current age makes this so encouraging and very appealing at a superficial level. But the inner despair I felt over a meaningless world without God was unbearable. Slowly I became more serious in my engagement both in heart and especially in mind.

Our parish offers many learning opportunities for growth, and I would try to take advantage when feasible. A few years ago, my wife spotted in our parish bulletin an opening for a docent at the National Shrine in Washington, D.C. Although hesitant at first, I applied and got the position. It has been the very best intellectual and spiritual growth engagement gift possible. I no longer doubt my purpose: it's to love and know God as realized in the Mass and as beckoned by Mother Church.

WE WERE ASKED TO TELL WHY WE GO TO MASS. THAT'S A question I'd never really thought about. I suppose I began as a child because I was taught to by my parents as part of my Catholic upbringing. But in my mid-20's I drifted away from the Church. I just didn't feel any connections with God and felt I was being hypocritical in going to Mass. This lasted for forty years. And then the Lord called me back. Out of the blue.

I was driving down the street and saw a family walking to Church: a mother, a father and two children. Really a Norman Rockwell picture. At that moment, I felt empty inside....something was missing....something important. I needed to go back to the Church, to Jesus. I wish I could accurately describe how clear that message was. But there it was, nine years ago.

I saw a parish priest; he heard my confession and had me take communion the same day. It felt strange, but in a good way, to be back. After a few weeks of going on Sunday, I felt I needed more, a closer connection. So, I went to Mass three times a week and soon it was every day. Maybe that was because I had been away for so long that it helped make up for the lost time. I don't really know. But it felt so natural, so right. An empty space had been filled.

People who know I attend daily Mass think I'm so religious. But I don't feel that way. I feel like I am not religious at all. My mind wanders in church, thinking about silly, unimportant things. And between each decade of the rosary, I ask God to forgive my wandering mind. All I know is that I have found what is important, late in life to be sure.

So, I guess the answer as to why I go to Mass is the connection to God that was missing for so many years. When I commit a mortal sin, I feel so lost, so miserable. And then, of course, the wonderful feeling on being safe in God's arms again after confession.

There's a song, the title of which fits me perfectly, "Where could I go but to the Lord?" Indeed, where?

It sounds rather juvenile to say, at the ripe age of 48, that I go to Mass because my mom and dad want me to, but that's the heart of it. I'm not referring to my earthly parents when I say this, as I did not grow up in a Catholic home. Rather, my Father in Heaven and Our Blessed Mother, Mary, have been whispering, beckoning, and moving mountains to get me to Mass from the beginning of my life.

For a reason that is still a mystery to me, I was baptized Catholic as an infant. Sadly, it would be more than a decade before I even heard the name of Jesus, and longer still until I had the slightest idea of who He is and what He did for us. Physically, I was completely loved and cared for by my earthly family. Spiritually, however, it was as if I were wrapped in my baptismal clothes, bundled in a comfy basket, and abandoned at the steps of the Church. That could have been the end of me, but my Mom and Dad in heaven would not hear of that.

As I glance back at the 48 years between now and then I

am absolutely overwhelmed by the number of times I am vividly aware of Our Lord and Our Lady coming to my rescue. To name just a few:

- Earliest memories of my Grandmom reading devotionals and singing praise to Him while doing dishes.
- Missionaries in our neighborhood talking about a place called Heaven where people are saved.
- A curious stumble into a Catholic Mass with my cousin as a very young child.
- A wildly unlikely opportunity to attend a Catholic high school, leading me to the sacraments.
- An invitation to teach religious education, leading to a lifelong vocation as a catechist.
- A providential marriage proposal from a devout, Catholic man.
- A miscarriage that viciously tested, and then cemented, my Faith.
- Strong Catholic women mentors, many of them.
- A painful, unanswered prayer that initiated a devotion to praying the rosary daily.
- A job that encouraged prayer, study, and daily Mass attendance.
- A call to serve in the Legion of Mary - a call to deeper conversion.

Every day I think about that baby's soul (my soul) abandoned at the church steps. And every day I think about Our Lord and Our Lady, "Mom and Dad," plucking me from the basket and bringing me inside - leading me to the altar - saving my life. Sometimes I cry with gratitude for the gift of the Mass and my life in the Catholic Church. And sometimes, in the weight of my humanity, I can barely drag myself out of bed to get dressed and go to Mass. It is in those moments especially, that I remind myself of the millions of ways that Our Lord and Our Lady have opened the doors of the Church for me and brought me to the altar to receive Jesus and give myself to Him.

That's the heart of it. Jesus saved me. He has shown me again and again, that He wants me there with Him. Every day He calls me to Himself in various ways. I am no longer a helpless baby, so I will run to Him. As long as the Good Lord allows me, I will go to Him at Mass. I choose life with Him, because He chose me.

WHY DO I GO TO MASS? MASS SAVED MY LIFE. IT GIVES ME food for the journey. I meet Christ there. I have to start my day with Christ or it is empty. I didn't always believe this or feel this way. It has been and is still a journey; one that I will continue until I see Jesus face to face.

When I was small, I sat on the kneeler and fell asleep in Mass. When I was a teenager, I sang in the teen choir, but felt the most important parts were the songs and the readings. Overall, I felt it was boring. I just didn't get it. Later, I was married through a Justice of the Peace to an abusive man against my mother's warnings. I knew he was THE one. My mother told me I was an adulteress for marrying a divorced man outside the church. I was convinced I knew better. My husband and I went to Mass, but eventually we stopped as the beatings got worse. It wasn't until I found refuge sleeping in the back of the church, tired and broken that I found my way back to Jesus and the church. I left my husband, got a divorce, and I started anew with my two children. Eventually, I had a lovely life with a new husband, four children and twenty years in the Air Force. I went to Mass daily and was in the Sunday choir, but I still didn't get it.

I was proud; overly confident in me, myself and I--MY

trinity. I was distracted in prayer and felt I needed to learn how to meditate, to keep focus. I joined Dahn Yoga. I knew I was strong enough to keep my faith and perhaps even convert them with my shiny example. What a fool! The exercise and meditation made my body feel good and they taught love and happiness. We were going to heal the world. I strayed once more and I became a Dahn Master. I was still going to Mass on Sundays and singing in the choir, but I felt sad because I didn't see the joy people should have if Jesus was truly present. In my mind, THEY were lost, and I was convinced that I was living the life of Christ as a Dahn Master. After all, I was healing people on a regular basis with my energy healing sessions. I had the most popular class and the most clients. I sympathized with fallen-away Catholics. In fact, they made up 80% of my clientele. I opened two new studios for Dahn. I was their "model" Master.

However, after three years, I lost all the joy I thought I had found. I was working from 6:00 a.m. to sometimes 2:00 a.m. the next day. I seldom saw my family. Dahn focused on drawing in Catholics…making fun of them. They put more and more emphasis on cash flow rather than the love and happiness I had bought into. In fact, I felt like an empty shell, tired and sad. I had neglected my husband and family, all for a company that was looking for the bottom line. The day I left Dahn I was so weak I could hardly walk. I left a note saying I was going back to the Catholic Church. I don't remember the drive home from Bethesda, MD to Fairfax, VA. I praise God for my Guardian Angel. Dahn Yoga hounded me for two months, wanting me to come back. But I was back home to a husband who gently took me back; to a church that gently took me back; to a God who gently took me back. It took time to learn more about my Catholic faith and why Mass and the Eucharist are so important as its center point.

I truly believe that continuing to go to Mass saved me from spiritual destruction. Even though I was unworthy; even though I was going astray; even though I was talking down about the church – through it all, God was trustworthy and helped me climb out of the hole I dug. Sometimes we need a kick in the butt to wake up and move upward.

So now I attend Mass daily to receive food for the journey which gives me strength, keeps me on the straight and narrow path, gives me inner peace and provides me with a community of believers to relate to and to depend on. Why is it different than before? Now I know: I get it and I hope to keep it. My hope is in Jesus who gave His life for me, and I'm giving my life to Him.

WHEN I WAS A TEENAGER I KNEW GOD WAS REAL, BUT I NEVER felt that close to Him like my grandma did. At the age of 18, I decided to look for God in other religions. I thought I found Him in the evangelical church and stayed with them for 10 years. Curiously, I never stopped praying to Mary because of my grandma. She told me that even though I was leaving Catholicism I should always respect Mary because she is the Mother of God and our Mother. I kept those words in my heart.

When I married my husband, I returned to my faith's roots: Catholicism; but I still wasn't very involved in the Catholic church until my children were born. In 2013, God blessed me with a gift: attend the daily Mass. My company transferred me from D.C. to Crystal City and my new job was three blocks from Our Lady of Lourdes. A week after I started my new job, I began attending the 6:45 a.m. Mass; since then, I haven't stopped. During the pandemic God had another gift for me: St Mary of Sorrows celebrated Mass every day and had the Blessed sacrament exposed from Monday through Friday.

Why attend daily Mass? God has found me. I was looking

for Him during my youth and He found me. He has made many changes in my life, and He will continue changing me. One huge change is my desire to attend Mass every day to receive Him in the Holy Eucharist where He and I are in a common union. I voluntarily receive Him with an open heart, with the desire to do His will.

I love Him because He loved me first. He shows me His love in the cross; through His blood He saved me. I believe He died for me. I believe He took my sins. I believe one day I will be in His presence face-to-face.

God gives me strength and I realize my faith is stronger. When I listen to the Scriptures and the homily, I pay attention because God is talking to me. I have a personal relationship with Him. Don't you want that too? Nothing is the same when you know Him, when you talk to Him. It took many years of my life to get to this point; now, I am the happiest person.

Why don't you try and give Him a chance? God is real. He is a gentleman. He will not do anything that you don't allow Him to do in your life. Now is the time. Do it...come to Mass...tell Him you need Him...and let Him do the work in you.

I was raised a Catholic and went to Mass every Sunday and on Holy Days of Obligation until I went on active duty with the United States Navy following my graduation from college. That was when I started to fall away from regular Mass attendance. I like to think that it was because we rarely had a priest available to celebrate Mass when we were on the ship, but I must admit that I didn't make an effort to go while in port either.

Then on April 12, 1970, I happened to be driving by St. Augustine Church in Newport, Rhode Island, and I noticed that the next Mass was going to start in ten minutes. In a spur of the moment, I parked the car and went in. Five days later, I had a date with a woman who would become my wife, and I've been going to church ever since. It's been more than 51 years of steady attendance, and I would like to note that on April 12, 1977, our third child was born. We now go to Mass not only on Sundays, but often during the week, to thank God for all that He has bestowed on my wife and me over the years. He is truly a loving God!

I ATTEND MASS BECAUSE IT MAKES ME FEEL CLOSER TO JESUS, reinforces my faith overall, and has helped keep me alive.

I was born into Catholicism and attended Catholic schools in New Jersey through the 6th grade until we moved to Northern Virginia. I was an altar server and memorized my Baltimore Catechism.

Upon moving to Annandale in 1970, I went to public schools, but remained active in the church. In the mid-70's I embraced the faith and under the mentorship of a parish priest entertained becoming a priest. He helped me gain admission to St. Mary's Seminary in Baltimore, but when push came to shove, I opted to head to Charlottesville and attend UVA.

I attended Mass on and off during college and that pattern continued after graduation. Not surprisingly, foregoing Mass tracked with troubles I was having personally, and I just could not put two and two together.

Over the next 40 years I professed to being a Catholic, but I was not practicing as I should. Finally, about six years ago, I got it. My life was crumbling around me. I was essentially dead: physically, mentally, and most importantly, spiritually. I got on my knees and prayed and found the strength to right the ship and returning to Mass was the lynchpin.

Since then, I have become active in the parish. I do so by

attending daily Mass, serving as an usher, co-chairing a ministry, and participating in the Knights of Columbus. Attending Mass really does serve as the bread of my life. It provides me with the time and place to stop and reflect. It helps me understand what is important in my life, generate the mindset I need to attack the day and allows me to recognize that I need to turn things over to God and that it is His will, not mine.

So, while I enjoy the fellowship that attending Mass provides, the driving force for me showing up at Mass is personal and truly lifesaving.

I WAS BORN IRISH CATHOLIC. MY FIRST TIME OUT OF MY house was to be baptized. We went to Mass as a family growing up pre-Vatican II. I think I can still respond to certain phrases in Latin. At five years old my brother and I belonged to a children's choir. My best memory from that time is singing "Ave Maria" with all my heart and being treated to a Coke at the Bride's wedding reception. My best memory from my first communion was feeling so holy that day and I liked my dress and veil. I loved feeling loved and belonged. I don't remember my first confession. As I continued to grow up, we went to CCD on Saturday mornings and Mass on Sunday.

Then my family stopped going to Mass. When I was in junior high, I begged my mom to go to CCD for my Confirmation. When I was in high school, I became a lector. When I was in college and after college, Mass was not important. I met my Navy husband and we eloped, but it was important for us to have our marriage blessed in the Catholic Church. So, we have two wedding anniversaries. Early in our marriage we didn't go to Mass because we had a boat and water skiing was more fun! We were first stationed in Japan and because my husband was out to sea, I went to Mass; it was something to do.

When we were stationed back in the U.S., we lost our first baby. It was a sad time, and we went to church to be comforted. But Mass every Sunday was not as much fun as water skiing. Several months later I was pregnant again and delivered a beautiful baby boy! Still, going to Mass was not important.

Two years later when I delivered our second beautiful son, a priest walked into my hospital room and the Holy Spirit whacked me in the head and heart. It was so clear to me that I wanted to raise our son as a Catholic. In wanting this for our sons I was given a gift. I fell in love with the rosary, our family enjoyed participating with the many activities our church sponsors, and I enjoyed becoming involved with the different ministries offered. We found a great church where we felt loved and belonged. I was building a gradual love for Saint Mary of Sorrows and its community.

I am not a perfect Catholic, not quite a saint, but with our Blessed Mother's intercession and more help from the Holy Spirit, becoming a saint will happen. Our sons are out of our house now. I am still discovering the many treasures of going to Mass at Saint Mary of Sorrows. I am praying to become the best Catholic woman, wife, mother and grandmother despite my Irishness. Going to Mass on Sunday calms me and reminds me to love each other as I want and need to be loved and belonged.

I grew up Catholic and went to church on Sundays, but I did not have a personal relationship with our Lord. I walked away from the church for a long time as a young adult. When I had children, I came back to church. But I still was not connected to my faith.

At Mass one Sunday, the priest talked about how God meets us where we are in life and wants a relationship with us. He loves us unconditionally! That changed my life. I had not felt worthy of His love and shied away from Him because I felt that God could not love me, as I am a sinner. I realize now that Satan plants those thoughts within you to keep you away from God. God showed me that He loves me and I need to look to Him, ask for forgiveness and move on by keeping my eyes, heart, and soul focused on Him. I still feel unworthy, but now I look towards Him.

Mass helped me to establish my relationship with God. Reading scripture and learning prayers helped me grow in my faith. Initially my faith grew slowly, and I could feel God leading me into a deeper relationship with Him. It starts with trust…trust in the Lord's love and guidance. Just look to Jesus and He will guide you, no matter where you are starting.

I'VE BEEN A RELATIVELY RECENT 6:30 A.M. MASS ATTENDEE. I have four kids; you've talked football with a few of them over the years. In response to your question as to why folks attend daily Mass:

I'm 57 years old and was raised Catholic. I had 12 years of Catholic education including four years of Jesuit high school. Like many, I strayed from the church in my early 20's and college, somewhat returning when I had kids. I've continued to be a Sunday Mass only person, and not always as regular as I ought to be. I went to church because I had to, not really because I wanted to.

This past February we had an incident with my 20-year-old that really made it clear that many things in my life are outside of my control. Out of desperation, I decided that maybe daily Mass might help. I started going and realized it really helped me recalibrate my focus. I've continued going for the past nine months because it's a great way to start the day and focus on what is important. It seems like a cleansing experience. For the first time in my life, I'm going to church because I want to go instead of because I have to go. It's a liberating feeling. (Sorry that it took so long to get to this point!)

When attending Mass weekly, I found it to be a nice recalibration to set things straight for the week. But I've come to realize that I need this recalibration daily (probably even more frequently!).

WHY DO I COME TO MASS? THAT'S SUCH AN INTERESTING question, and it's one that required considerably more introspection than I initially anticipated.

If I'm completely honest, my first answer, of which I'm neither terribly proud nor impressed by its superficiality, is basically, "I come to Mass because I've been told since I was a child growing up in the faith that that's what I'm supposed to do. Simple as that."

But as is the case with many questions of consequence, there's more to it. Like lots of young people, when I was in college and probably for a few years thereafter, I drifted away from making Mass any sort of a priority. For starters, my mom wasn't looking over my shoulder, making me feel guilty about not going (which numerous punchlines suggest is a mandatory skill set for Catholic and Jewish mothers alike).

On top of that, during those years I also started wandering a bit aimlessly in terms of my spiritual life. Some would call it "finding oneself," but looking back that's probably too generous, too noble sounding a characterization. In fact, I was treating my relationship with God like the process of selecting a neighborhood in which to live. I wanted comfort and safety—well, sure, who doesn't? But I also wanted convenience and a relationship that would...meet **my wants, my needs** and most importantly that would do so on **my terms**.

With the passage of years, life did what life does. It threw at me a succession of scarier and scarier situations that left me completely overwhelmed...concerns about illness, employment, family relationships and a host of others. Each and every single time that happened, I found comfort in my true north...in returning to Mass...experiencing the Eucharist...spending purposeful, focused time with the Maker of the Universe, who also quite incomprehensibly knows every hair on my head...every burden that haunts me and every joy I celebrate in every moment of my life.

I come to Mass because I find things there which I find nowhere else. I find peace, wholeness, connectedness, and quieting serenity—things against which the modern world rages at every juncture...things without which the human soul withers like a flower petal in the sun.

Do I make it 100 percent of the time? Nope. Truth be told, I'm not sure I could name more than half of the Holy Days of Obligation. But that's the gig. I'm terminally imperfect. Nevertheless, every time I come back, the doors are open, and I'm welcomed. I'm forgiven for my failures, and above all I'm loved...perfectly. I can't imagine life without that Gift, that respite, that sanctuary.

That's why I come to Mass.

BACK IN THE MID-60's, I LEFT THE CHURCH BECAUSE OF THE changes that transformed the Catholic Church as a result of the 2nd Vatican Council called by Pope John XXIII, now a canonized saint of the Catholic Church. The Church's Mass went from Latin to English. The bishop ordered that our little Historic Church's altar be torn down and the new version of the altar, which faced the people, replaced the old altar. My

People, who were daily communicants, went to attend the first daily Mass after the modifications. We were all devastated when we saw the new changes, and then we left the Church.

For the next 25 years, I did not go to Mass or receive the holy sacraments. Throughout this period, I felt lost and felt like there was something missing in my life. I didn't know what it was. One day when I was on my way to work, (I always left early so I could get things organized before the workday started), I drove by this Catholic Church, which I had not ever noticed before; it was named St. Elizabeth Ann Seton Catholic Church. I stopped and looked at it remembering the days when I attended Elizabeth Ann Seton Hospital's Medical Laboratory Technician Training Program. I remember one of the nuns asking me why I did not attend the early morning Mass, because I was always so early for classes. I told her, "I don't go to Mass anymore because it's not in Latin."

While the early Sunday morning Mass was going on at St. Elizabeth's, I opened the door and heard the Choir singing, "Here I Am, Lord. Is it I, Lord? I have heard you calling in the night. I will go, Lord, if you lead me. I will hold your people in my heart." I burst into tears as the people were receiving the Holy Eucharist and the Choir kept on singing. I sat down in the back row crying. I couldn't receive the Holy Eucharist because I'd been a non-practicing Catholic for so very long. After Mass, I sat there crying and when the Priest was coming down the aisle, I went to him and said, "Father, will you hear my Confession?" I was still crying, and he said, "Yes." After my Confession, Father went to the get the Ciborium from the Tabernacle, opened it and brought me the Holy Eucharist. After that, my whole life changed, I began attending Mass on Sundays, and Daily Mass when I was not working.

Today, I make a strong effort go to daily Mass because He, Our Loving and Kind Lord, called me. It's very interesting that one time in a dream I was called by name and asked to take my place. I didn't know what was going on and I was scared because I was asked to step out into the void. Then I heard His voice again, He said, "Where is your Faith?" I stepped into the void and walked to the altar where I received Him. It was this experience that solidified my return to the Holy Mass and now Holy Adoration, where I pray, talk to Him and sing His holy praises. On my way to Mass and Adoration, I say, "Here I am Lord, I come to do your will!" Not too long after this event in my life, I went home and my brother introduced me to his friend, who made such a huge difference in my spiritual life. It was she, by the Grace of God, who truly brought me back to the Holy Mass, and then later I became a Secular Carmelite. Through God's workings I saw, heard and felt His presence in the Eucharist. It was then that I knew He truly dwelt within me.

Finally, I come to Mass daily to repent for my sins, to ask for forgiveness for my failures and faults which crucified my Dear and Holy Lord who died for my sins! When I enter His church, I begin with the Act of Contrition, which I say every night before I sleep. While at Mass and on Adoration, I pray that the Lord helps me to keep His commands, and to live faithfully my perpetual vows of Poverty, Chastity, and Obedience, especially through the Beatitudes given to us by **Our Beloved Lord Jesus in The Sermon on the Mount**. As I call Him "Blessed," I pray that He may one day call me "Blessed" for all eternity. "Sacred Heart of Jesus, Have Mercy on Me."

I WAS BORN AND CAME OF AGE BETWEEN VATICAN II AND JOHN Paul II. I went to Catholic schools for elementary and high school and I received all of my sacraments. My family went to Mass on Sundays and Holy Days. I served as an usher and a lector.

Unfortunately, the Church did not seem to be firmly grounded during this period, and, as a consequence, I did not receive a firm grounding in the faith and definitely was not told about God's desire to have a personal relationship with me. When I left my parents' home and it was my turn to decide if I would go to Church, I decided I would not. As the saying goes, a well catechized Protestant becomes a Catholic. A poorly catechized Catholic becomes a Protestant. While I still called myself a Catholic, I wasn't following the faith.

In my 20's, I was rudderless. I went to Mass sporadically – when I visited my parents, Christmas and Easter, on random Sundays when a feeling came over me. Mostly Sundays became a day to sleep in, read the paper and meet friends to eat brunch or watch football. A boss at this time was sending his children to the Catholic school so that they wouldn't be tempted to join a cult. I was still at least a nominal Catholic and thankful that I wasn't tempted to join a cult.

I married in my 30's. We were married in the Church, for my father's sake. While I wasn't a regular church goer at this time, I told my husband I wanted to raise any kids in the faith, so they wouldn't join a cult. My husband, a lapsed Catholic himself, agreed and we began attending regular Mass.

Approximately 10 years later, my husband was sent to Iraq for a year. I was not happy about this and prayed that God would "fix" it. He did not fix it in the way I wanted. He fixed it by calling me to serve the Church. I received a call from our DRE asking me to be a Catechist for the 2nd graders. I didn't feel qualified to lead a class in a sacramental year but agreed to teach 3rd graders. That led to more than a dozen years as a catechist with more than half of that teaching Confirmandi. To teach the faith, I had to learn the faith and the Lord brought me deeper and deeper.

The more I learned, the more I desired to grow closer to God. The closer I grew to Him, the more He asked of me and the more blessings he gave to me, primarily in the form of my parish family. I found myself going to Mass because I wanted and needed to be with God and his Church.

I would like to experience a flashy Eucharistic miracle because they are cool, but I have been blessed to experience tingly Eucharistic miracles. When the priest raises the host, when the bells ring, when I ask God to only say the word and my soul shall be healed, my body tingles. I know I will be receiving Jesus, and through the Most Holy sacrament, He will be strengthening me for the next task He has for me. I go to Mass to visit my friend, our Lord, to be strengthened and to show the world that I am a part of the Body of Christ.

I'M NOT SOMEONE WHO LIKES TO GO ANYWHERE VERY MUCH. When I was deciding to return to the Church after 22 years, weekly attendance felt like a big commitment. While I love Mass now, and usually attend more than once most weeks, on some Sundays I think that I pray better at home alone, or that I focused better watching Mass on the livestream (which is a large part of how I became interested in returning).

But that greater focus I enjoyed during the livestreams enabled me to develop a better understanding of what's so special about Mass. I hadn't fully appreciated that we are praying with the angels and saints until I listened more closely to the prayers. Being in a church filled with people praying along with Heaven is an experience we can't get at home. Since God also comes to us in the Eucharist, regardless of how long we've been away from Him, or the previous sins we've committed, I don't want to miss an opportunity to experience that closeness with Him, and thank Him for his constant love and forgiveness.

When some of the enthusiasm I felt upon first returning to Mass starts to wear off, I remind myself that the reason I did return was probably very simple and hard to refuse: He asked me to.

I AM A SINNER. PERHAPS NOT A SPECTACULAR ONE, BUT ONE who has routinely failed "in my thoughts, in my words, in what I have done and in what I have failed to do" in living up to the ideal given to us by Jesus of Nazareth and His Church.

Mass has always been part of my effort to be the best person I can be, to overcome my weakness, and to stay connected to God in a distracting and overwhelmingly secular world. I would hate to think who I would be without it.

I grew up in a family of practicing Catholics and attended Catholic schools from first grade through my undergraduate years. For much of that time, it was just normal for me to attend Mass. I had a sincere faith as a child; Mass was important to me, and I felt safe and comfortable there. As I went through my turbulent adolescence and the social upheaval of the late sixties and early seventies, I continued to attend Mass, but being a practicing Catholic became much less comfortable. Looking back, I believe I developed something of a "bunker mentality" about my faith, and clung stubbornly to my practice of attending Mass, even while I struggled with self-doubt, negative peer pressure and a desire to fit in with others who scorned what I grew up believing. My "bunker mentality" ended only after a failed relationship left me shattered and questioning everything in my life; I felt as if all certainty had abandoned me.

As I put myself back together over several months, with the help of my family and a good psychotherapist, I saw many things clearly that I had never admitted to myself — how I had hurt others, how I had fooled myself, even how I had used my faith as a crutch. I came to a point where I could see how all religious faith might be self-delusion; I peered into the abyss of life without my Catholicism. In that moment of crisis, by the grace of God, I chose my Catholic Faith and made it freely and permanently mine. One of the key turning points in that process happened at Easter Vigil Mass, when the image of the Lord rising from His tomb hit me with great force and helped me know that I could follow him out from the dark place where I had entombed myself.

For me, there is no Christianity without the Eucharist, without Mass. I could never be a Protestant; if I did not believe, as the early Church did, that the Eucharist is the real presence of Jesus Christ, then I would conclude that Christianity itself is just another mythology.

So why do I go to Mass? Because it is my anchor. It allows me to separate from my noisy life in this noisy world, to remember who I am and what I believe; to partake of that greatest of gifts, the Eucharist, and to do so in a community of fellow believers. In the presence of the Eucharist I can find peace and clarity that eludes me elsewhere. Mass feeds my soul and allows me to hope. Not being able to attend Mass in person during the pandemic left a void I could not fill. To paraphrase St. Peter, to whom shall I go, if not the Lord at Mass?

As I tell my children, there have been many times in my life when I did not feel like going to Mass; there has never been a time I have regretted going. I have attended Mass in foreign countries with languages I did not understand, but it was still recognizably and spiritually the Mass. I have attended Mass during the lowest times in my life and Mass has been central to many of the happiest events of my life. When I go to Mass, I am going home.

Some Additional Thoughts

After we had published the hard-copy version of the "Why I Go to Mass" book, we were asked if we would be willing to take some more parishioner inputs. Our answer was: "Sure"!

We hope these latest reflections are as of much interest and value to you as are the "original" ones.

— ST. MARY OF SORROWS PARISH
COUNCIL

To help me discern my ability to stay on the path to heaven, and the actions I need to take to guide my family and others to life eternal in heaven.

...BECAUSE I HAVE NOTHING TO LOSE AND EVERYTHING TO GAIN.

I attend Mass because my faith is the foundation for my life. At Mass we are in the true presence of Our Lord Jesus Christ, present in the Blessed Sacrament. That is such an awesome gift that we have. Attending Mass is so important; this was instilled in me as a young child. I am so thankful for that and hope and pray I can instill that in my children's life. I am so blessed to have a supportive spouse. Yes, there are times during Mass when the children get shaky and I think "please relax" but we are so lucky to have parish priests who are patient, kind and understanding. Jesus has protected us and kept us safe in good times and through trials that we all endure.

During overseas deployments, Mass was not always available due to a shortage of chaplains, and I felt so abandoned. I was yearning to receive Jesus. I am not perfect and I think that being with Jesus helps me to grow stronger. I have been lucky to have been protected even after falling.

I mentioned I was raised in a devout Catholic family in the Philadelphia area. My sister and I were always being "shuffled" to various Novenas (e.g., Miraculous Medal, or Lady of Mount Carmel, and St Joseph) with our mom and grandmom. I feel so lucky in Philadelphia to have had Saint John Neuman and Saint Katharine Drexel as role models; reading their lives has helped me to understand charity and Eucharistic Adoration. At times we were "bribed", but I truly now know that helped us. This is a tradition I want to be able to (God willing) have with my children and spouse: going to novenas and visiting the Poor Clares.

My mom would always pray when there was something that needed to be turned over to Jesus and Mary's intercession. I would truly say it was my mother who instilled this in us and it was through her example.

We are so lucky to have all that at our Parish offers spiritually; most importantly, the daily Adoration. That "saved" me and my family during COVID. We were so lucky to be able to go to church daily as well as have weekly confession, even though Mass was not available. Also, we were lucky to have been able to visit the Poor Clares. Our priests and our Bishop deserve SO much credit for allowing that for the parish. That to me was so admirable and I will never forget them for that grace and for being so good to my family. They are very accepting and we need to pray for them daily.

WHILE RECENTLY LOOKING AT THE PICTURES IN MY OLD HIGH school yearbook, I was filled with memories realizing everyone's unique personalities and interests. How and when and why did this uniqueness happen? This uniqueness happened at the moment of conception when the uniqueness of the mother and the father became a separate unique being. Each of us is created by God with an immortal soul and a God-given mission – a service to God that no one else can accomplish. This mission may be minor in nature, or it may be one that could affect our community, our nation, or our world. Each mission, large or small, is equally important to God. At the end of our journey here on earth, we hope to hear, "Well done, good and faithful servant."

Be assured that we are not alone in accomplishing this life's mission. God has given us a unique set of strengths, weaknesses, and the ability to realize our strengths and overcome our weaknesses. At the same time, however, God has also given each of us a free will which can direct us along a path we fashion ourselves or along the path He intended. Before we stop to bemoan our abilities - wanting more - or weaknesses - wanting fewer, remember they were given specifically to us by God; and He does not make mistakes.

The world today presents many life-style images to which

we can aspire: star athletes, popular celebrities, worldly successful individuals. It is easy to be influenced by other people or someone presented in the media. It is easy to use this free will and fashion a path to "fit in" with today's culture.

Following the path God has intended is not quite so easy. It does require help, not from popular accolades, but from being in the presence of Jesus. He will help us. Yes, we do need help and guidance. We can sit down at the piano, but can we learn to play the piano without a personal teacher? Can we learn to paint without some personal guidance? Remote learning simply whets an appetite and eventually frustrates us. There is no substitute for direct personal contact. At Mass the priest, acting in the person of Christ, consecrates the Host with Jesus' personal Presence. When we consume that Host, Jesus becomes part of us. We strive for our will to conform to His will. When we go to Adoration before the exposed body of Christ or reflect in front of the tabernacle, we allow His Presence to come into our minds and hearts.

Just going to Mass or Adoration is not the solution by itself. Playing the piano takes practice. Painting takes practice. To pray takes practice. There are many prayers we have memorized, but do we truly absorb their meaning, or do we just recite them? For example, do we reflect in the Our Father on the words "… Father … Thy name … Thy kingdom … Thy will …"? To absorb the Mass takes practice. This practice includes study, meditation, and reflection. When we take the Host into our body, do we realize Jesus has become one with us? By opening our hearts and truly realizing His Presence, we are directed along the path He intended utilizing our unique abilities and fulfilling our unique mission in life.

It is easy to forget that each of us has a guardian angel who monitors us throughout the day and night. Our angels are given to us by God at conception and are with us until death. Unfortunately, our guardian angels are frequently ignored. They try to guide us; but their voices are quiet, and we may not be paying attention. When we have a sudden thought and say to ourselves, "Hey, that's a good idea," there is a probability our angels had a hand in that.

Guardian angels are constantly in the presence of God; so, has your angel given a good report to Him? Your angel, however, cannot go to Mass alone. What a wonderful treat it would be to take your angel – to witness the consecration – to see you become one with Jesus – to feel your peace. So … take your Guardian Angel to Mass.

It's very hard to put into words why I go to Mass, but I'll give it my best shot. I remember one parishioner answering this question by saying "because it makes me happy", and I always liked that response. Why do people believe; what makes people have faith? I think only God truly knows the answers to those questions. I can start by telling you a bit of my story. I am a cradle Catholic because of my mother, a devout Roman Catholic raised in the Philippines. I was baptized, had my First Communion, but never went to Mass regularly as my mother often worked several jobs at a time and was a single mother of three kids. Growing up, I felt at home at the Catholic Church, I liked the priests, liked the sacraments, loved receiving the Eucharist and feeling at peace afterwards. I remember attending a Chinese Protestant church for a short time as a kid, as there weren't many Chinese Catholics in the area, and even as a nine-year-old, noticing all the differences to my Catholic parish.

When I graduated high school and left for college, I was ready to get as far away from home as possible, and attending Mass was probably the last thing on my mind. And so it went into early adulthood. I was always a "good person" who tried to do the right thing, but sorely lacked a strong religious foundation. I remember driving by churches on Sundays, seeing people stream out of their houses of worship, and thinking I was missing something, but never thinking about going to church myself. After all, most of my friends weren't religious; and again, so long as I was a "good person", what was the point in going to Mass?

In my early thirties, however, I had a series of personal crises, which would be too lengthy to get into, which essentially made me realize I was not as in control of my life as I had thought. I think it invariably happens to everyone: at some point you have a realization that "your way", no matter how well-intentioned, is failing you. In my case, I thought I had life figured out, and had my own "rules" as to how to live my life. Little did I know my way was like a house of cards, built on a shaky foundation, just waiting to collapse.

So, I started attending Mass again, had an emotionally draining confession after a nearly 20-year absence, met monthly with a non-Diocesan priest, read Scripture, finally received the Sacrament of Confirmation that I had missed as a kid, and slowly started building up my spiritual life again. One thing that astounded me was how easily I went into my "prayer space" after receiving Communion again, the feeling I had when receiving First Communion as a child had stayed with me.

So, what now? Is life perfect after finding my way back home to the Catholic Church? Not by any means, but it feels great to journey through life with God by your side. God was always there, even when I had lost my faith, but now I am embracing him back. And that is why I go to Mass.

✠

I go to Mass because my grandparents were Catholic and my parents were Catholic and they raised my siblings and me to "be" Catholic. Being Catholic meant going to church on Sundays and holy days of obligation. It was just what we all did.

Along the way, the institution of the Catholic Church started letting me down: the disdain for many segments of God's population, the relegation of women to second class member status, Vatican banking scandal, and the sexual abuse scandal with its lies and protection of priests rather than victims. Baptisms are invalid because a priest said the wrong word? Value the unborn but not the LGBTQ? It is becoming more and more difficult to reconcile priests and bishops wielding power to punish those not in lockstep with their narrow vision, with Christ's embrace of sinners while they were still sinners. What has happened to the big messy Body of Christ Catholic family? And yet I still go to Mass despite these failings of the Church as an institution.

It was only when I stopped expecting the Church to do or be anything for me, and decided to go to Mass to worship God, that Mass became relevant again. This is my chance to sit/stand/kneel in awe of the majesty of God, and express it in song and prayer within a community of believers. It is no longer about what did I get out of that sermon, but instead about what do I bring today? Do I bring my failings, sorrows, and woes to the foot of the cross? Do I bring my gratitude and joy to the feast at the table? Do I bring my unsettled mind and sit in silence before my Creator, offering even that back? The Church may disappoint, but the hour in praise with God never does. And that is why I go to Mass.

Because it is an essential part of my life. The Sacred Heart of Jesus and the Immaculate Heart of the Blessed Virgin Mary are engraved in my heart!!

Attending Mass is a precious way and opportunity to thank God for everything and for the Diving Love we received in Holy Communion! Amen.

I go to Mass because I notice my week is better even when there is a lot of chaos. It's the same peace I receive by saying the daily rosary: my day is better. I don't know why that is, it just seems to work out that way. Mass is a place where I leave the rest (or, at least most) of the world outside the doors and feel at peace. The church is the only place where I feel that way.

Being a Cradle Catholic I was brought up to go to church because I was told to. Now that I am older, I go because I want to. When I am at Mass I feel at peace. I like receiving Jesus in the Eucharist. I also like the community. I am also an altar server. That role helped me get close to Jesus. I feel close to Jesus at Mass. During COVID I started to watch it online. I like it online, but I didn't get the same feeling as I do of going in person. I still watch daily Mass online just because I can get there. I go to Mass because it brings me closer to God.

As a cradle Catholic, I grew up knowing it was expected that I go to Mass every Sunday and holyday of obligation, and was encouraged to go to Mass other days, schedule permitting. As an obedient child, I followed that expectation – and still do. While it seems to be a shallow reason, establishing this habit has sustained me through the "dry times" of my faith journey. As I grew and matured, I found other reasons to go to Mass.

I go to Mass to participate in the sacrifice of the Mass. When the Vatican II-generated changes to the Mass started, I was not quite ten years old and I was enthralled by being able to participate in the responses to the Mass. This was transformational; I went from being an observer ensuring I was in the right place - reading the English on the right page by following the Latin on the left page - to being a participant! This participation figuratively gave me a front seat in the sacrifice of the Mass. One example is during the Gospel on Palm Sunday and on Good Friday, when we say, "Crucify Him! Crucify Him!". I face my personal culpability contributing to Jesus' passion and death; I can't ignore it as something that happened long ago, but instead face it as one who needs a Savior. My participation was the start of my active role in the life of the Church.

I go to Mass to worship my Lord. I was fortunate to have experienced both the original Tridentine Latin Mass, the transition Masses, the eventual post-Vatican II Mass, and the most recent translation. Each provides a different perspective that adds to the richness of the Mass. I see that when I go to Mass, I am transformed through my upward connection to Jesus and my connection to everybody at Mass with me – and everybody who has ever participated in the Mass. This elevates worship to a relationship not only with God, but also with the entire body of Christ. When I see Jesus – in a freshly consecrated host – elevated for all, we are worshiping our Lord, and it moves me in a particularly special way.

I go to Mass to worship my King. As Americans, we don't often think about our relationship with our King, because we have no earthly relationship with a human king. Yet, we look at the tabernacle, Jesus' home on earth, and it's fit for a king. I am His subject, and he is my King who wants the best for me. being in relationship with my King touches me and is a source for meditation.

I go to Mass to share in worship with everybody there and those who in the larger communion of worshipers throughout history. My worship at Mass is enhanced by others, as we are worshiping together. We are a community. We support each other. We inspire each other. I think of an old woman attending Mass with me several decades ago, whose face was transformed to beauty when she received the Eucharist, because she was with her Lord. I meditate upon that transformation and the beauty of someone who loves Christ. The community we build at Mass extends beyond that – after Mass, supporting each other, and even beyond our church community, because Mass challenges us to reach out to others in community. Further, sharing in the Mass throughout history connects us to an unbroken tradition over the centuries of those who have ever attended Mass. That strong connection with all the saints before us provides inspiration and help.

I go to Mass to be uplifted by the beauty of the worship space. We build churches that are inspirational; every church can inspire us. Sometimes it's easy to find the inspiration, such as in the mosaics at the Maria Laach Abbey in Glees, Germany, or in the baroque design of Melk Abbey in Austria. Gothic churches are particularly inspirational to me, and I can think of many. Yet, I can find inspiration in modern churches, too; they provide a contemporary enthusiasm for our Lord. I even found inspiration in a very humble church, a converted garage where people would drive up to an hour to get to the nearest Catholic church, because the parishioners found it important to band together to build the space and to make it part of their life.

I go to Mass to be fed with the Word of God. This is one of several places where I learn more about my Lord and my faith, and I continue to find new insight each time I revisit a reading; the message in the Bible is both universal and time-less. I am very grateful for our cycle of readings and liturgical calendar, which set the cadence for the Word of God over time. I love how the readings build on each other throughout the week and each liturgical season and year. I love the antici-patory mood of Advent and the somber, penitential mood of Lent – and how they prepare us for the absolute joy of Christmas and Easter. I love the Triduum, how it brings us through the first Eucharist, into the Passion of Good Friday as we face our sinfulness, and culminating in the Easter Vigil as it brings us through salvation history to the Resurrection.

I go to Mass to be fed with the Eucharist. While we can be intellectual and learn about God through studying the Bible, the Eucharist is where my relationship with God is reinforced. Jesus is my Lord and He cares so much about me that He wants to be this close with me! This experience enlightens my knowledge and brings it to a relationship.

I go to Mass to pray and to meditate. While we can pray and meditate anywhere, going to Mass provides me with a rich environment for prayer where I can focus on Him without the constant distraction of daily life.

I go to Mass to renew my desire to live my faith as best I can and to strengthen me to face life's challenges. That hour at Mass grounds me in my faith and reminds me that I cannot just live life as I wish, but that I must strive to accept God's unconditional love for me, to strive to be pleasing to God, and to share that love with my fellow man. It is too easy to lose sight of that in daily life; I need to be strengthened.

In summary, I go to Mass because I need it. I need rela-tionship with my Lord, the communion of saints, and my parish community. I need the inspiration of the worship space and the Word of God. I need to worship. I need the teaching. I need its encouragement to reach my potential as a Christian and as a human. I need to be fed. Mass provides this for me.

WHEN I WAS SEVEN YEARS OLD MAKING FIRST COMMUNION AT St. Charles Borromeo Church in Pikesville, Md, I was in the pews reserved for my class. I did all the "ups and downs" required of good Catholics during the Mass. A great light enveloped me and I stood transfixed looking at the altar and the cross. I felt such warmth and wholeness. Apparently my continuing to stand when all others sat brought distress to the Sisters of Charity who educated me. They descended on me to "please sit". I did, but I was different.

From that day on I had a personal relationship with God. My faith was everything. I credit this to keeping me a virgin when I dated hordes of guys and was really enjoying life.

After marrying the love of my life (a gift from the Blessed Mother), our faith held us close. However, it was still "God and Me". In 1975 I made a Cursillo which smacked me in the head. It wasn't just about "God and Me" but about the community of saints that God surrounds us with every day. Once I was just a vertical believer - God and Me. Now, I had to add the horizontal beam of the Cross. I had to have community with others who also loved God as I did.

So, I come to Mass to embrace a community of believers. I celebrate with them. Each Mass I meet someone new, and oh how happy I am. We are brothers and sisters in Christ.

I GO TO MASS BECAUSE THERE IS NOWHERE ON EARTH THAT I would rather be. My first-grade teacher and my parish priests must have done remarkable work in teaching me to love Holy Mass and to wait with the greatest joy for the moment when Jesus would come to me in "Holy Communion"! I have never forgotten the "Prayer Before Communion" that we memorized and prayed aloud with such love just before the Sacred

Moment! Perhaps you remember it, too! "Oh my God, I believe more firmly than if I saw it with my own eyes, that it is Yourself that I am now going to receive in this adorable Sacrament!

I believe it because You have said it, and You can neither deceive nor be deceived. Oh my God, I love You! Pardon me for having offended You. Mary, my sweet Mother, lend me your immaculate heart, that I may love more worthily your Jesus and my Jesus! Your God and my God! Oh, my dear Guardian Angel, watch over and protect me at this important hour!" Over the years, I myself have prepared hundreds of children to receive the Sacraments. What a blessed privilege and awesome responsibility!

At each Holy Mass I pray that every mother and father, lay teacher, sister and priest will have many blessed opportunities by their words and by their lives to lead the children to love the Holy Sacrifice of the Mass, to cherish the Holy Eucharist throughout their lives until they see Him FACE TO FACE.

All Are Welcome!

"Peace be with you. As the Father has sent me, even so
I send you."

— JOHN 20:21

Here are some resources that we use in our parish that you may find helpful for deepening your faith life: **Formed, Word on Fire,** and **Institute of Catholic Culture.**

FORMED: The Catholic Faith. On demand.:
https://formed.org/

WORD ON FIRE: Proclaim Christ *in the* Culture:
https://www.wordonfire.org/

INSTITUTE OF CATHOLIC CULTURE: Know the Faith. Love the Faith. Live the Faith.
https://instituteofcatholicculture.org/

IF YOU ARE A NON-CATHOLIC OR UN-CONFIRMED CATHOLIC adult interested in looking into the Catholic Faith, each local parish has a program called the **Rite of Christian Initiation of Adults** - better known as the R.C.I.A. This beautiful program talks about what the Catholic Faith is and why we believe the things we do.

The Rite of Christian Initiation of Adults at St. Mary of Sorrows Parish:

Do you know of a non-Catholic family member, friend, neighbor, colleague who may be interested in knowing more about the Catholic faith? Do you know someone who was baptized Catholic, but has not received the sacraments of Eucharist and Confirmation? Do you know someone who has been coming to Mass for a while, but is not Catholic?

The St. Mary of Sorrows RCIA team is waiting to warmly welcome all who may be interested in learning further about Catholicism. We will guide inquirers on their journey to a deeper faith, and, hopefully, full communion in the Catholic Faith.

For more information or to register, please contact Father Barkett at 703-978-4141, Ext 103

CATHOLIC DIOCESE OF ARLINGTON

ARE YOU LOOKING FOR GOD?

Do you have questions about your self-worth, forgiveness, or the meaning and purpose of your life?

Do you have questions about religion, the existence of God, the identity of Jesus Christ, and the teachings of the Catholic faith?

Do you wonder why Christians are so divided and what is unique about the Catholic Church?

Do you have a hunger to know about the Church Jesus founded, and to know the truth that He promised will set you free?

Are you interested in learning more about the Bible?

Do you want to know how to pray, and what it means to live as a Christian?

Were you baptized Catholic but never received First Communion or Confirmation? Are you a baptized Christian interested in becoming Catholic?

For more than two thousand years, the Catholic Church has safeguarded and handed down to each generation the fullness of the Christian faith, making Jesus Christ present in every time and place and inviting all to know and follow Him. We invite you to bring your questions to Jesus, confident that He will answer through the Church He left us. Healing, forgiveness, and peace are available to you in the Catholic Church. Jesus is knocking -- will you answer?

If you have immediate questions or would like some help on your journey of faith, please contact us!

https://www.arlingtondiocese.org/becoming-catholic/

Behold, I am with you always to the close of the age.

— MATTHEW 28:20